Have Bible Will Travel

*Dedicated to my wife Audrey and our three
wonderful children, John, Ruth and Joy.*

Have Bible Will Travel

AN AUTOBIOGRAPHY

BY PETER ANDERSON

AMBASSADOR INTERNATIONAL
Greenville, South Carolina • Belfast, Northern Ireland

HAVE BIBLE WILL TRAVEL

© Copyright 2009

NB. Unless otherwise stated, Bible text and quotations are from the NIV

ISBN 978-1-84030-208-0

Ambassador Publications
a division of
Ambassador Productions Ltd.
Providence House
Ardenlee Street,
Belfast,
BT6 8QJ
Northern Ireland
www.ambassador-productions.com

Emerald House
427 Wade Hampton Blvd.
Greenville
SC 29609, USA
www.emeraldhouse.com

List of Contents

Foreword

We are living at a time when we seem to be knee deep in people's 'life stories' either serialized in the popular press or published as full blown books. Most of them come from the shallow end of society and deluge us with details of the writers' experiences as pop singers, film stars, 'media personalities', sporting heroes and the like. Reasonable cases can be made out for some of these, but the whole thing becomes laughable when the author is in his twenties. One British footballer recently signed a five-book deal worth £5 millions over twelve years. The first ghost-written instalment, with the trivial title *My story so far,* hit the market when he was barely out of his teens but was launched with his claim that 'it will be good for people to see the other side of me.'

The book you are holding is different. Peter Anderson is a rightly respected evangelist, tested and tried over five decades of faithful Christian service throughout the United Kingdom and in many countries overseas. Nor is there any commercial motive behind the writing of the book. Suddenly hit by a life threatening accident, his public ministry seemed over, but superb surgery from a surgeon from an overseas country saved his life. Confined to his home for four months as he recovered, he decided to write something of his life story regardless of whether it would ever by published, 'as an exercise in tracing God's goodness, not least in giving me so many opportunities for ministry over the past five decades.'

Peter Anderson has a memory that would make the idiomatic elephant seem forgetful. In a story that takes us to every part of the United Kingdom, Eastern and Western Europe, South America, Africa and Asia he recalls in sparkling detail incidents that point to God's providence and protection, the power of the gospel and the working of God's grace in the lives of believers, especially those living in situations where their faith placed them not merely in difficulty but in danger. I shared his early visits to Greece and to what was then Czechoslovakia and reading his accounts of some of those visits(replete with holy and humorous details that had long ago left me) has been especially meaningful. Since then, his extensive ministry in Bulgaria has been remarkably fruitful and his memories of over thirty visits are among the most moving parts of the book.

Unlike the sporting tyro, there is 'no other side' to Peter Anderson and in these pages he takes us artlessly through some of the highs and lows, delights and disappointments, accidents and illnesses that he has known. Youth work, evangelistic missions, conferences, radio and television work and ministry in myriads of settings from pulpits to prisons (including Singapore's notorious Changi Gaol) are all reflected here as is the remarkable way in which he started from scratch and with the expertise of the Christian Television Association produced a series of highly effective missionary films for UFM Worldwide.

Yet evangelism runs in his veins and he could not resist ending the book with a gospel message, one that precisely reflects his preaching - clear, concise and Christ-centred.

'Have Bible – will travel' left me cheered and challenged; I hope you will share my experience.

Dr. John Blanchard

1

Early Days

Life began for me in Glasgow where my father was a 'regular' serving in a Scottish Regiment. When his regiment moved on, so did we as a family. During the first ten years of my life we moved at least 6 times from places as far away as Kilmarnock and Portsmouth. During World War II my school was evacuated to Brockenhurst in the New Forest. This was early preparation for later years as an itinerant evangelist.

My mother was a committed Christian, and I owe so much to her example and her prayers.

At the age of 18 I received call-up papers for National Service and joined the army. As I had previously worked in the finance office of Portsmouth City Council, I was placed in the Royal Army Pay Corps, and after six weeks of intensified training was posted to Singapore.

We sailed from Southampton on the 'Empire Fowey,' which was to be my home for the next six weeks. Before we reached the Isle of Wight I learned the horrors of sea-sickness and took a long time to recover. It was a fascinating journey, going through the Mediterranean, the Suez Canal, the Red Sea, Aden (now Yemen) and the Indian Ocean. Once, when hit by a terrible storm, many of my fellow soldiers felt as I did. That this was nearly the end of the world as the ship rolled drunkenly from side to side! It was a great relief to reach Colombo the capital of Ceylon(now Sri Lanka) where we were able to spend a day ashore - our first experience of an Asian city.

I soon became aware that my Christian faith was not experimental and in reality I was no different from the other 18 year olds on board -1500 of us! The words of the gospel I had known from childhood, but had no inner knowledge of the Lord Jesus Christ in my life.

God, however had not deserted me and even on the troopship He reminded me of Himself. One evening, I heard hymn singing coming from one of the upper decks. On investigation I found an army major leading hymn singing, many of which I recognised.

On arrival in Singapore I found myself in an office looking after the pay of the Gurkha soldiers. Also in the office was a soldier I recognised from our basic training in Devizes. I knew that he was a Christian, but as he slept in a different barrack room from me I could ' escape' from him out of office hours! I couldn't escape from God —He was still stirring my memory.

David was persistent and sought at work to build up a relationship through our joint love of sport. The Gurkhas were mad about hockey, and we quickly learned to play this 'ankle bruising' game, and to make friends, with these very tough soldiers.

Singapore provided many experiences for us, and whenever my army pay allowed it, I would go down into the city to enjoy myself.

David sought to share his faith with me on many occasions but must have been in despair at my refusals to go with him to meet some of his Christian friends at the church he attended. He challenged me to read the New Testament for myself, but I refused though I could see how much his faith meant to him. It was not for me.

I have since learned, in the words of the poet Francis Thompson, that the 'Hound of Heaven ' does not give up His chase very easily. In Psalm 139:7 we read 'Where can I go from your Spirit ? Where can I flee from your presence? If I go up to the Heavens you are there. If I make my bed in the depths' you are there.'

After six months in Singapore, I was due for two weeks leave so planned to escape from Christian witness! I chose to get away to the army leave centre on the Island of Penang off the North Coast of Malaysia. At this time we were fighting a war with communist guerrillas who were hiding in the jungles of Malaysia. Our train journey from Singapore to Penang took us through this area, so we had an armed guard of Royal Marine Commandos, and we also were armed in case the train was attacked. Twenty four hours later we arrived at the town of Butterworth and from there across to the island.

The army leave centre was very comfortable and provided all that we needed for rest and relaxation. While swimming one morning I bumped into 'another soldier' and apologised, only to find that I had actually bumped into a large turtle! There were many fascinating things to see and do. On my agenda was a visit to the snake temple! In the capital Georgetown, there were dozens of restaurants, a cinema, night clubs and the 'Happy World Park.' Here you could buy vouchers, hand them to one of the 'Hostesses' who would then have to dance with you. Not a lot of fun for me as I have 'two left feet.'

One very hot afternoon, I walked into a cinema where it was cool, without first looking to see the title of the film being shown. It was 'Samson and Delilah,' a story in the Bible I knew well, which told of the disaster that will follow someone who knows the truth but choses to ignore it. Each time I went into Georgetown, the bus went pass the Penang Gospel Hall with a gospel text on the notice board.

Two week laster I returned to Singapore, to the office, and of course to David. It was the Easter weekend. On Sunday evening David found me feeling miserable and sorry for myself. I had spent all my money while on leave. He asked me about the leave centre, and then invited me to come with him to a youth rally at his church on Easter Monday morning. He added as 'bait', that after the rally he would take me out to the 'Stamford Grill,' one of the best steak houses in the city at that time. I'd once looked at the prices on the menu and hurried past.

Because I was so fed up I said yes, thinking that I don't have to listen to the speaker, but will enjoy the steak! I didn't realise that David had enlisted some of his Chinese friends to pray for me. Those prayers, combined with 18 years of prayer by my mother were about to be answered.

It was eight months since I had entered a church, and I was amazed to see that it was packed. We managed to find two seats on the back row, but I felt very conspicuous as it seemed that we were the only non-Chinese there that Monday morning. The preacher was a Doctor Benjamin Chew. In one sense he said nothing that I had not heard before, but this time it seemed different. The Holy Spirit was convicting me of my sin, and Christ was telling me to stop running away from His love. At the end of that service, during the singing of the final hymn I cried out to God in my heart to save me and to forgive my sin and rebellion.

David kept his promises to take me to the steak house and it was only on our way back to camp that I told him I'd become a Christian. He then told me how his Chinese friends had been praying for me. He helped me tremendously during those early days of my Christian life, encouraging me to read my Bible and to witness in the barrack room. They asked me where I was now going on Sunday mornings, and I was able to explain that I had become a Christian and wanted to meet with other Christians. They never gave me any aggro when they heard this, though there were occasionally some amusing incidents. One night I returned to barracks after lights out, climbed into bed only to find it was full of empty beer bottles!

Through the years I have learned that good foundations laid down early in life will stand you is good stead later. My mother laid those foundations, now David was underlining them. He also introduced me to two lovely Asian Christians who were to greatly influence me as they showed me the importance of the Bible in my life. They also taught me that though I was a new Christian, I was called to take the gospel to others. These aspects are just as important in the 21st Century as they were in the 1950's.

My first Asian mentor was an Indian whose name was G.D.James, an evangelist with the Brethren. His influence stretched to many other Asian countries. Many weekends I stayed in his flat, little knowing that while I was there he and his wife slept on the floor while I slept in their bed!

I will never forget his advice to me concerning Bible reading. When you read your Bible, ask yourself three questions. What does it say? What does it mean? How does it apply to me? You can find out what it means very easily - read it. Let its message soak into your heart and life. He also told me to try and memorise verses of the Bible. Write them out on small cards and stick them in your uniform pockets.

Some parts of the Bible that you read may be easy to understand, but others not so easy, so you need to ask the Holy Spirit who inspired the Bible to help you in this department. Don't worry if sometimes you do not get the whole meaning at first reading, keep on, and the next time you read that verse or chapter it will be clearer.

He then underlined to me, just how important it is to ask yourself 'How does what I have just read apply to me?' Fifty years later I still use these questions and find them so helpful.

My second mentor was a young Chinese evangelist, Robert Tan by name. He was only a few years older than me, and from the word go he encouraged me to get involved in evangelism. I went with him on some of his evangelistic ventures and slowly but surely I found myself involved on a personal level with preaching the gospel in a simple way. The Gospel Hall in the city had a Sunday night after church evangelistic service and as many servicemen would pass the hall, they could be invited to come in for tea or coffee and a mound of sandwiches. As those giving out the invitations to come into the hall were mainly very attractive Chinese young ladies there was always a good number of servicemen that came into the hall!

I had only been a Christian for about 6 months when Robert told me that on the first Sunday of the next month I was to be the preacher. I nearly died of fright and spent hours praying and preparing an evangelistic message on the words of Jesus in John 3:36. 'So if the Son sets you free, you will be free indeed.' Robert introduced me and I lasted all of 9 minutes – and had to have three closing hymns to spin out the time! Robert was so encouraging, and said that even though I only kept speaking for such a short time and quoted yards of Scripture, that it was the Word of God and the Holy Spirit could make that Word travel down into the hearts of those who were listening.

At this time there had been a take over by communism in main land China and all missionaries had to leave. Many of what was then called the China Inland Mission landed up initially in Singapore, and one of these was a fiery American missionary named Paul Contento. I loved to hear him preach the gospel in Mandarin, even if I could not understand the language. I could feel a sense that God was speaking to his hearers. One day he asked me to come with him down to Chinatown where on a Saturday night we would give out large Chinese poster tracts in the market.

Some of the young people from the church who came out with us thought that they might be able to teach me to sing a simple gospel song in Chinese. The words were very easy. 'Come to Jesus, come to Jesus, come to Jesus just now. Come to Jesus, come to Jesus just now. Come to Jesus just now.'

I practiced over and over again, both in private and to the young people of the church until they thought that it was just right. Down to the market we went and as someone started to play the simple melody on the little pedal organ, my gospel singing career started. Alas it also finished quickly. Yes I drew a crowd of amused people, but Chinese is a tonal language and I had got it wrong. Instead of singing 'Come to Jesus just now.' I was singing 'Come to Jesus for salted vegetables.' I drew a crowd as they wanted their share, and my singing career was at an end!

There was another occasion that I will not forget. At the start of the Korean war, many of our army units on their way to the warfront stopped off in Singapore for further training. Most of these soldiers were National Servicemen – possibly feeling very scared at what awaited them. There was a NAAFI club just across the road from the famous Raffles Hotel. Robert Tan and some of the young people told me that on Saturday night we would go down near the NAFFI club and have an open air preaching of the gospel to the soldiers from the Gloucester Regiment as they came out of the club.

When the meeting got under way, Robert turned to me and said, 'Peter, I want you to speak next, they will listen to you because you are a soldier like they are. So it was, that with a Bible in my hand and feeling very nervous I preached the gospel for the first time in the open air. They did listen well as Robert said they would. The regiment went on to Korea and as we know they were decimated and most of them never returned alive to the United Kingdom. I have often wondered how many of those young soldiers were hearing the gospel for the first time and certainly many of them for the last time. It certainly impressed upon me how important it was to preach the gospel whenever the opportunity was given.

Now my time in Singapore was coming to an end. Three more months and back to the U.K. and demob from the army. Back to being a civilian again. However there was one more challenge that I had to face before that glad event. The church that I was now attending in Singapore was going to have a special Bible Convention and an American Bible Teacher was coming from the States to preach each evening for a week. I planned to be present as many nights as possible. On the last night instead of preaching the gospel, he challenged us to seriously consider the call of God to service for Him on the mission fields of the world. As he finished preaching I felt that God was calling me to make myself available to him for wherever He wanted me to go and whatever He wanted me to do. The preacher gave a simple invitation to the audience of mainly young adults to come and stand at the front as a confirmation and a testimony that you were willing to be available. I stood with them.

As I made my way back to camp that night on my own I had a real assurance that God had some ministry for me in the future, but that first of all I must get some Bible College training to equip me for that ministry.

As I was on the other side of the world, I knew nothing about Bible Colleges but I managed to pick up in a Christian bookshop a copy of a British Christian Newspaper. In it I read an advert for Redcliffe College. I hastily sent an airmail letter to the Principal applying to study there. Alas it was not to be, the Principal replied telling me that Redcliffe at that time was a ladies only college. Although some of her young ladies wished that men were allowed to study there!

In my letter to the Principal I had told her that I was feeling that God might be calling me to be an evangelist and she replied suggesting that I might write to Frederick Wood the founder of the National Young Life Campaign because they had a training college for evangelists. So I sent another airmail and again was disappointed when a reply came back to say that the college was now closing, but that Matlock Bible College in Derbyshire might be suitable as they trained evangelists. At this point I felt that it was wisest to continue in prayer and wait until returning to England before pursuing this third Bible School.

As usual, it was a hot steamy January morning when I embarked on the Empress of Australia for the four week journey back to Liverpool followed by a train journey to Portsmouth and home.

2

Back Home to the UK

The day after my return home the church held a Friday fellowship meeting that had been started during the war mainly for servicemen. The Pastor asked me to share my testimony after a young lady had given hers. As I stood to speak, she hurried out of the building. Later, I learned that she was a student nurse and due to be leading the Nurses Christian Fellowship meeting that she had recently started. Little did I imagine that one day she would become my wife!

It was now time to contact Matlock Bible College (known now as Moorlands). On writing to the Principal, he replied with a very warm letter saying that they would be very happy for me to come and study with them. He ended the letter with the words 'Faithful is He who calls you, who also will do it.' (1 Thess.5:24.) The following Sunday a visiting preacher took those same words as his text, which I accepted as confirmation from God, through His Word, that Matlock was where I should study.

My friendship with Audrey was growing, as we both felt that God was calling us to His service, possibly together. During the summer evenings when she was not on duty, we would stroll along Southsea promenade, always ending up at the famous free speech site to support the missioners of the Open Air Mission. It wasn't long before they asked me to share a brief gospel message.

Two very fruitful years followed at Matlock Bible College. It was good to be in the company of other young men who felt called to evangelism, and also a Principal who had been an itinerant evangelist before starting the Bible College.

As well as studying the Bible, most weekends were spent in outreach evangelism. Many Saturday nights I stood on the other side of the road, opposite the cinema in Matlock as people queued up to see whatever was being screened that night. We would preach the gospel and offer a booklet that explained more of the Christian faith. Sunday meant getting on the bike and heading out into Derbyshire, and sometimes further afield to preach in one of the many small village churches.

Every year we had a special College outreach in an area of the country where there was a good local church that could organise and make use of 12-15 students. This meant visiting homes and speaking to people, a nightly meeting for children and possibly a youth rally on the Saturday night. If there was a free speech area in the town then we would preach in the open air.

One night in Macclesfield I was asked by our team leader to give a short gospel message. In those early days I tended to go like an express train when preaching. The local Pentecostal minister suggested that 'I had been quickened,' to which our Team leader said, 'But we are asking the Lord to slow him down!'

At the end of each College year, if you were physically fit you had to go on what was called a College Trek. The Principal said that it was good missionary training. If you managed to last six weeks then you could say that you thought it was good training for donkeys!

Each team of eight pulled a wooden covered hand cart fixed to ropes at the front and the back. Four of us were attached to the ropes, two on either side and then two on each side of a handle in front so that the cart could be steered. The last two were on bicycles and every one had a turn on the bikes. The cyclists would also go ahead on our journeys and find the church hall where we were going to eat and sleep, and have at least two meetings each evening. Into the cart went all our clothes and cooking utensils.

My first trek was from Matlock to Portsmouth, walking every day between 10- 15 miles, but stopping each weekend at a church. In the middle of this period we reached Southsea on the South Coast where we were going to stay for a week of open air meetings at the free speech site on the promenade. It was the week of the review of the fleet and so Southsea was packed with visitors.

Part of the purpose of these treks was to teach us what it meant to rely upon the Lord for all that we needed during the six weeks. The College gave us what was then a ten shilling note, and no student was allowed to take any personal money. We were not to ask any church for money and we had to feed ourselves on all week days, but could accept invitations for dinner on a Sunday. Of course, many churches and individuals en-route would give us food or provide a meal, but we were never to ask for it. It certainly taught us to pray, and very wonderfully God always provided sufficient for our needs. Here again it laid down good foundations of trust in God for future ministry wherever it might take me.

There was one amusing episode in a Hampshire town. We arrived at the church late in the afternoon having been on the road since breakfast. Our advance guys on the two bikes had put the large kettle on for a welcome cup of tea. The church caretaker provided us with tea bags and milk and then said that in the garden at the back of the church there was a lot of rhubarb and that we were very welcome to help ourselves to it. It was an interesting meal before our first meeting that night! Stewed rhubarb for first course and also for the sweet course, and then it was stewed rhubarb for breakfast before setting off on the long walk to our next destination. As you can imagine there were many stops en-route and we vowed that we would never touch rhubarb again on this trek!

Our trek at the end of the second year was from Matlock to Blackpool with a week of mission by the sea. It was like being back in the army again where at basic training camp you really became fit. It was also good training at getting on with other Christians at close quarters. We all had to take our turn at cooking food – and some of the dishes produced were certainly interesting!

Our cart was nicely painted and we were allowed to take basic clothes as we did our own washing on the journey. So where did we sleep? In church halls in sleeping bags, and you soon found out that if it was a Baptist church then over the baptistery with some give on its cover was by far the best place to sleep. After a busy day walking and pulling the cart with maybe two meetings in the evening there was little difficulty in sleeping.

Blackpool was very different from the previous trek to Southsea. Here we had a wonderful 'Good News Hour' on the sands for children, and most mornings we would have about 100 boys and girls of all ages. Many parents also sat on the sand getting a sun tan and listening to what was being said and sung. David Iliffe, one of the team who later became the founder of 'Children Worldwide,' usually spoke at this, but one morning asked me if I would do a flannelgraph story of Zacchaeus from the New Testament. I had just put Zacchaeus on my board sitting in the branches of a tree to watch as Jesus was passing by. Suddenly there was a strong wind, Zacheaus was blown away down the sands and a small dog who appeared to be listening chased after my flannelgraph figure and I saw him no more! The children of course were highly amused, but Dave never asked me to do the children's talk for the rest of that week!

Blackpool is a fascinating place and in the summer months is teeming with people, all of them wanting to have a good time. There is nothing wrong with that. However behind many a smiling face there was an emptiness, and we came across this late at night after our open air meetings on the beach.

It was here in Blackpool that we tried a new method of encouraging people to stop and listen. Ron Burton was our team leader and he was a good evangelistic preacher. He would stand down on the sands and start speaking. I would stand up on the promenade and as people passed I would start to question Ron, and so would start a two way conversation as the gospel was brought out from what the Bible says. People always love an argument and so every night it drew a crowd. At some point in this backwards and forwards conversation I would say to Ron that I did agree with what he was saying and was asking the questions that people standing with me on the promenade wanted to ask. There was never a night when there were not a lot of good conversations with people about the gospel and we knew of some that professed faith in the Lord Jesus Christ and subsequently we were able to link some of these folk with evangelical churches in their home towns.

One evening we were very surprised when three attractive young ladies joined in with my questions to Ron. When I said that I agreed with all of his answers they joined in and said that they did as well. Talking with them afterwards they told me that they were part of a dance group at one of the Blackpool Shows on the Pier, and had been converted early in the season at a special evangelistic show business meal.

On the way back from Blackpool the team thought that I was in an unusual hurry, and then when I wanted to leave them a day before the trek finished they had the answer. I was heading down to Romford in Essex to marry Audrey. So I basically left college one day and was married the next. So began our 52 years of marriage and service for God. Yes, I had the Bible, was confident of its message, and I had a great desire to bring its message, the gospel of the Lord Jesus Christ, to people wherever and whenever I could meet them.

More changes

During the second year at Bible College and preaching most Sundays in the village churches of Derbyshire, plus several college missions and treks I found myself drawn into closer fellowship with two other students. We often met and prayed together about our future ministry. One evening the Principal invited the three of us to his office, Ron Burton, David Iliffe and myself. He said that he wanted the three of us to be responsible for a special college mission. He didn't know at this time that we were praying much about the three of us working together as an evangelistic team when college days were over. We felt that this invitation was the assurance we needed that this was what God was calling us to do. When we told the Principal, all he said was, 'Praise the Lord.'

It was now 1954 and the Billy Graham Harringay Crusade had made evangelism front page news, not only with the general public and the media, but churches all over the country were waking up to the challenge of reaching their communities with the gospel. One of our last outreaches before the end of term was in Hull where the church were having sound relays from Harringay. What the organising committee did was not very wise. They had Billy Graham by relay one night, and the next night it was me –live. You can guess what happened. For the Billy Graham relay the church was packed out, but by the next night when I was preaching there might have been about 100!

Talking with Christian friends and with our home churches, we decided that we would call ourselves 'The Crusade for Christ Team –Three men, One message.' It was not that we only had one sermon and shared it between the three of us, but rather that we were three men with the one message – the gospel.

On our two six week treks from college we had been introduced to many different churches, and with evangelism now at the fore front of church thinking after the Harringay Crusade, our diaries began to fill up with invitations for evangelistic missions so that it really was 'Have Bible –will travel.'

For the next five years we travelled up and down the country gaining invaluable experience in preaching the gospel, both in church buildings in the winter and on the beaches and in tents during the summer months. We attempted things then in order to reach people that I don't think I would have the courage to do today. From standing on a fish box on the quay at Whitby, to going into a local dance hall to see if I could speak in the interval. The manager was speechless and I think was about to say 'no.' when I butted in and said, 'Has somebody been here before ?' He gave me permission and as the band struck up 'When the saints go marching in,'I stepped onto the dance floor and briefly shared the gospel. As I finished I saw a girl looking very distressed and then going towards the door and out. I quickly followed her and found her outside crying. She was a Christian who had decided that she stood more chance of finding a boy friend in the dance hall than in her church. The last place she thought she would be reminded of God was at the dance.

One cold February we were conducting an evangelistic mission in an Anglican church in a small Yorkshire town. One evening, we jointly felt that we were to have an open air meeting in the Town Square. It was very cold and it did not seem a sensible thing to do. I was standing shivering listening to my colleague speaking, and to be honest I hoped that he would soon finish so that I could get back in the warm. To my horror he said ,'And now my friend will speak.'

For some strange reason we were standing outside a butcher's shop with a large posted advertising 'Tripe for Sale.' A few people hurried past and then a well dressed lady carrying a violin case came round the corner and stopped in her tracks and started listening intently to what I was saying. When I had finished I gave an invitation for any one who might be interested to ask for a booklet explaining more of the Christian message. The lady stepped forward, asked me for the booklet and then told me an amazing story.

She had been to an orchestra practice that evening but never came this way home until that night. Over many months she had been listening to a Christian radio programme on Trans World Radio, and the speaker's name was Stephen Olford. The messages so moved her that she decided she would go to church the next Sunday. Sadly, the message was not the same. She had tried three different churchs, and had nearly given up when on this night she came right out of her normal way home, heard the message and sought the Lord.

What an open air meeting that turned out to be, and what a crowd! One listener, but with a heart prepared by the Lord. We all rejoiced as we returned to the warmth of the church hall, but I had to confess to the Lord that I hadn't really wanted to be out in the open air on such a cold night. Sometimes I wonder how many other people there are in our world with hearts prepared by the Spirit of God to receive maybe the last link in the chain as that woman did so many years ago.

I am always challenged when I read the story in Acts 8 of Philip and the Ethiopian Chancellor of the Exchequer. It is the story of a Christian man who when told by God to do something made himself available to God. The story goes like this. 'An angel of the Lord said to Philip, go south to the road –the desert road that goes down from Jerusalem to Gaza. So he started out, and on his way he met an Ethiopian eunuch, an important official in charge of all the treasure of Candace, Queen of the Ethiopians. This man had gone to Jerusalem to worship, and on his way home was sitting in his chariot reading the book of Isaiah the prophet. The Spirit told Philip, go to that chariot and stay near it. Then Philip ran up to the chariot and heard the man reading Isaiah the prophet. 'Do you understand what you are reading?' Philip asked him. 'How can I' he said, 'unless someone explains it to me?' So he invited Philip to come up and sit with him. He was reading what we now know to be Isaiah 53, and after he had read it he asked Philip, 'who is the prophet talking about, himself or someone else? Then Philip began at that very passage of Scripture and told him the good news about Jesus.' And the outcome was that this high official was converted and went on his way rejoicing.

How did all of this happen? God said 'Go' to his servant Philip and he went. There was no argument, no discussion, just obedience. There is an important Biblical principle here and it is that obedience to God always brings blessing to us and nearly always brings blessing to others. This remarkable story in the Acts of the apostles is a story of a man who made himself available to God and God led him to one whose heart was already prepared like the lady in that small town in Yorkshire stopping to listen to the message of salvation and forgiveness on a cold February night.

3

Moving On

Five very exciting years of evangelism in our country were coming to an end. David Iliffe was moving to full time evangelism with children, eventually founding an organisation called ' Children Worldwide.' Ron Burton was called into pastoral ministry and I was invited to join the staff of the National Young Life Campaign as their home and southern counties evangelist

Y.L. as it was known was founded by the Wood brothers, Frederick and Arthur Wood. Their objectives were to reach the young people of our country with the gospel and then to see them discipled and harnessed to youth evangelism, both in their local church and then into small YL groups across the country.

In this early days of YL the Wood brothers must have held evangelistic campaigns in most of our major cities. Today I live in Leicester, and remember talking with F.P.Wood one day in his flat in London as he told me of a 4 week mission in our De Montfort Hall(the largest hall in the city.) He said that he preached every night there for 4 weeks, and that in those days there was no amplification !

As well as evangelistic missions, Arthur Wood produced a hymnbook and Frederick wrote a number of books, all of them out of print today. One of his smaller books was called 'Questionable Amusements. The Y.L council asked me to re-write it which I eventually did, but gave it the title 'Suicide on the Instalment Plan.'

During the summer months, camps for children and houseparties for teenagers were held. The teenage houseparties were handed to Audrey and myself to be responsible for. Audrey looked after the administration of these, including seeking out large boarding schools in different parts of the country and then finding the staff that we needed to take to each venue. Some years we had two hundred young people a week for four weeks during August which meant that over the years we had the privilege of ministering to about 800 a month. They had a great holiday while at the same time being under the sound of God's Word. Many were converted during those days and others were challenged to Christian service both at home and overseas. It was always a joy each week to have as our guest a missionary, or missionary family who were available to speak from the platform, or individually to young people.

Many years later having branched out to other parts of the world, I was due to go to Brazil. I asked the folk who had invited me if somebody would meet me at the airport when I arrived. Before going to Heathrow to catch my plane I still had no idea who would meet me. This was my first trip to Brazil so how would they know me?

Arriving at the airport, collecting my luggage and going through customs and immigration, somebody hurried across to me, greeted me warmly and took my suitcase, as he said with a smile on his face, 'You don't recognise me, do you ?' And I had admit that I didn't. He replied, 'I came to your houseparties for a number of years and during that time God called me to the mission field. I am now the Principal of a Bible College here in the city and we train Brazilian young men to be evangelists in their own country.'

Around the country at this time most of our major cities held 'Youth for Christ Rallies.' All of them were held on a Saturday night in Town halls hired for the occasion. Over a three year period I had the great privilege of preaching in at least ten of them and a number of times at what was called the Tent Hall in Glasgow. If ever I needed an underlining of my total confidence in the Word of God, and the gospel contained within its covers, it was surely during those many Saturday nights during the winter months.

During these years the Lord blessed Audrey and myself with three lovely children. We were living in Portsmouth within walking distance of our local church, and while I was away so much, Audrey began a ministry in our home. Many young people dropped in on Sundays after church, and also mid-week to do an Emmaus Bible Study course. There were several Christian sailors coming to the church and they brought some of their unconverted friends to the house.

Most of my ministry was with local churches and some of these were in very unusual places. In October 1960 Battisford Evangelical Free Church invited me to conduct a Crusade in Needham Market for three weeks. For a number of years they had been holding open −air services in Needham (about 5 miles from Battisford) and they longed to do something more solid. On hearing that the Secondary Modern School was only available at the weekends, the local vicar, Father Hargreaves Thomas, willingly allowed us to have all the weeknight meetings in the parish church that is sited on the main road running through the town.

Having been built in 1450, it was of some historic interest. G.H.Cook in his book 'The English Medieval Church' says, 'The climax of English roof construction may be seen in the astonishing roof of the Nave of Needham Market Church. It is one of the most sensational efforts of the medieval carpenter.'

I came all the way from Portsmouth on my Lambretta Scooter, parking it out side the church in plenty of time for the opening meeting. Turning the handle and opening the front door I was confronted with a card on the notice board bearing the inscription, 'Our Lady of Walsingam. Of your charity pray for the repose of the souls of,' – then followed a list of names of departed parishioners. Even more startling was another notice that said, 'In the most high sacrament of the altar, the Creatures of Bread and Wine, by virtue of Christ's words in the consecration are changed into the very body and blood of our Saviour Jesus Christ.'

Not the usual background for an evangelistic Crusade! Inside the church I was confronted with 8 small altars, countless candles, and over the High altar a banner with the words 'Blessed Sacrament We Thee Adore,' inscribed on it. As I was wondering what on earth I was doing there, the vicar walked in, greeted me warmly and told me that I was very welcome in the church to preach the gospel. but that he was going away for a holiday!

Night after night it was a great joy to preach the gospel in such a situation and to rejoice in the knowledge that some found the Saviour, both young and old, including the church organist. One other problem was the fact that a large grandfather clock was set in the wall beside the pulpit and it would chime on the hour. You had to be sure that you only reached the hour chime before the message, during the singing of a hymn, or about ten minutes after the conclusion of the last hymn!

On the second Sunday night, back in the Battisford church God worked in their own congregation in a remarkable way. The singing of the hymns was accompanied by a men's brass band and the conductor of the band was a young farmer from a very godly background. I have never kept a record of what I have preached on, but I cannot forget this night. I was preaching on the story of Cain and Abel in the book of Genesis and emphasising that with the same background and opportunity to go God's way 'Cain went out from the presence of the Lord.' It was a solemn message and after praying I announced the closing hymn. The band struck up an introduction as the conductor stood up to conduct them, but he could not do it and began sobbing like a baby. Other men came and joined him at the front and they were weeping. I sat down and could not close the meeting but took the young men down to the vestry at the back only to find another couple of young men. They had all been the subject of prayer, some for many years, and what rejoicing there was that night.

One young man told me that under deep conviction he had not slept the night before after being in the Needham Market meeting, and now he wanted to trust Christ as his Saviour. God even used the singing of a hymn to reach the heart of a young man in the Young Farmers club across the road.

Late night specials were held in the Institute Club and Corn Hall in Stowmarket, and hundreds of local teenagers were also reached with the gospel. I don't think that I will ever forget the Needham Market Crusade, the strange location in the church, or the remarkable response to the gospel from these farming young men in Battisford.

Tent Crusades

During the latter end of my NYLC days I planned a series of Tent Crusades on Southsea common with the big tent pitched within 200 yards of the fun fair and amusement park. There was no way that I could run these on my own, but there were other NYLC evangelists and so these Tent Missions were team events, with of course the commitment of young people who belonged to some of the YLC groups in Hampshire. As well as all that went on in the tent, for me it was also an introduction to reach out with the gospel into Secondary Schools, and this ministry would continue for many more years in the future. On my first morning assembly in a local school, Helen Shappiro who was Top of the Pops at the time was appearing in our City Hall. Her top song was 'Walking backwards to Happiness.' My morning assembly talk was on the fact that you can't walk backwards to happiness, but the Christian way to happiness was to be found in Jesus Christ. This may seem very tame stuff now, but then it was quite revolutionary to be able to preach the gospel in schools.

During the 16 days of Crusade we had 65 meetings in schools and some days there were as many as 7 school meetings. Doug Barnett my YLC colleague was introduced to one school assembly. Two hundred stayed to hear him speak for a further ten minutes! I was to follow this up with a request from the head asking if I would speak at a special meeting convened for 30 of the most difficult pupils of the school. Sixteen of them gave their names to the head later in the day requesting literature concerning what it meant to be a Christian.

During the second week I had an invitation to appear on Southern Television and quite a number of young people came into the tent as a result. We also heard of a prisoner in one of HM.Prisons to whom God spoke through the Telecast. 'Letter for Chipperfields Circus sir,' said the postman, as he cycled into the tent one morning. 'Sorry' we said,' wrong event.' 'How much is the show ?' asked the Teddy boy standing at the tent door one evening. 'What do you believe about the bomb ?' was the question from a group of CND adherents. 'Is there any beer left Jack ?' shouted the drunken sailor as he staggered drunkenly into the tent long after the meeting had finished.

Yes, they were all there on Southsea Common and around the fun fair and amusement park in a search for 'fun.' As the sun set over the western side of the harbour, the lights of the fun fair began to wink out their invitation to an evening of escapism. Many of these young people seemed to have no direction in life, but round and round in circles with no purpose but escapism. So many simply bound up in youth's eternal quest for happiness.

One night a young fellow came into the tent. He wore tight blue jeans a black jacket and had a great mop of untidy auburn hair. What first attracted me to him was the number of teeth missing from the front of his jaw. He had lost them in a drunken fight a few nights previously! Ricky was his name and I discovered that he lived in a one roomed flat with a fellow and his girl friend, a gas ring and a 21 inch TV set.

Ricky heard the message many evenings. One Sunday afternoon he collapsed on the common and was taken to his room. Too little sleep and food and too much to drink had caught up with him. He sent a message over to the tent asking someone from the tent to visit him. The next evening armed with a bunch of grapes Doug found his way over to the dingy cramped flat. The love and kindness shown to him seemed to overwhelm him – for he was a stranger to love. One night he returned to the tent and at the late night extra he said to me with real pathos in his voice, 'I wish I could believe, but I could never change.'

Then there were two girls who came in most nights. They sat in the front row and chain smoked all the way through the message. Motor cycle oil hung heavy in the air when the 'ton up boys' arrived. They listened respectfully and then shook hands as they left. Sailors, from broken homes came in on shore leave from the Naval boats tied up in the nearby dockyard basin. Sometimes they were the worse for drink and in an argumentative frame of mind. Teenage girls leaving the tent were asked why they were going so quickly and replied. 'You told us that the guy speaking was a young fellow. He must be at least 20!' Actually I was 30 at the time!

A Poem written by a 16 year teenager aptly summed up the emptiness of heart that so many of these kids were experiencing.

'A radio playing music – slow and sad.
Fitting for thoughts of sorrow and pain.
A drink smooth and potent
Slowly swallowing down the everlasting pain.
Cigarettes – one after another
Numbing the senses – keeping the mind busy.
But when the music is over – what then ?

I don't think that I will forget Barry. One afternoon I had a telephone call from the City probation department from one of the local probation officers. He told me that he had under his care a young man named Barry that he had seen that morning on one of his weekly visits as he was just out of borstal. The officer went on to tell me that Barry had told him that he had been coming into the tent mission and wanted his life to change. 'If I tell him to come down and see you, would you talk with him.' I quickly agreed and wondered who Barry was. The next night after the late night extra had finished a tough looking guy came down to the front and told me that he was Barry. He then told me an amazing story. Yes, he had been many nights in the tent and it was obvious that God had been speaking to him. His father had murdered his mother and he was living with his sister who was a local prostitute. He had been sent to a borstal institute because he had nearly killed someone while robbing him! He then told me that he could not sleep after his last visit to the tent, so he got out of bed, knelt down and prayed the Lord's prayer. It was the only prayer he knew. It was obvious that God had met with him and forgiven and saved him. For the remaining nights of the Tent Crusade Barry became our security guard and woe betide anybody who tried to damage the tent. One night I had to drag him away from somebody outside who was trying to loosen some of the ropes.

To my amazement after the mission was over he settled in a Baptist Church in the city(I think that there was some female attraction as well!) At a Christian Endeavour weekend he was asked to give his testimony by way of answering questions. The last one was, 'Has it made any difference to you since you became a Christian ?' to which he replied, 'It's made a hell of a difference.' The guest speaker took it up beautifully when he said, 'Yes, Barry is right. It has made the difference between heaven and hell.' Thank God that Barry wasn't the only one who found out that when the gospel takes root in the heart and life it is as radical as Barry had discovered.

Five years as a youth evangelist in the 60's were very formative in many ways. But I was beginning to feel that God wanted me to have a broader understanding of how to reach other age groups with the gospel. Just at that time and partly because I had been knocked off my Lambretta

Scooter by a drunken driver while on the Isle of Wight which affected my health, I was invited to be the assistant minister at a large church in Leicester. I was to be responsible for the youth work and also the evangelistic outreach of the church.

However shortly after arriving to take up this ministry, the minister was taken ill and I became responsible for all the preaching for nearly six months. Twice on a Sunday and Bible School mid-week. Sunday night preaching was always evangelistic, so this challenged me to go further in my study and preparation for 'Have Bible –will travel' that would take me to other parts of the world in the future. It was challenging and awesome as a young man of 33 to have a Sunday congregation of between 6-700 with whom to share God's Word. My heart though was still in itinerant evangelism, and after two years at Melbourne Hall I returned to this ministry.

Our three children were now at school. It was important that we should settle at a new church and find a house near enough, so that when I was away, the family could walk to church. While I was away Audrey searched for such a house and finally found one at the right price. It was about 400 yards from our new church where we have now been members for over 30 years.

During this time of waiting and praying I was approached by MWE (Movement for World Evangelisation) to become one of their evangelists, and so this was the next step into a wider ministry outside the United Kingdom as well as holding missions in the United Kingdom. It was good to be working again with other like minded evangelists, two of whom I would subsequently be involved with in many ministry opportunities in the years ahead.

As well as serving local churches in their evangelism we were involved in many team missions when a group of like minded evangelical churches would join together for a period of intensive evangelism. One such mission was at the invitation of the Island of Jersey churches for an 'All Island' Crusade when all sections of the Island Community were reached with the gospel. After an official welcome at the airport it was off to a reception at the Hotel de France.

Outreach opportunities were many throughout the two weeks. I was invited to speak on the dangers of the occult, at a meeting for policemen who had been involved in a recent occult case on the Island. Every senior school invited us during school time to speak at morning assemblies and then to stay on during the day to speak to classes. We had concerts in the bandstand in the central park and even on Channel Television late night epilogues.

Each night throughout the two week mission we had public meetings in the Spa Pavilion at 7-30pm and then 9-45pm for youth. Both meetings were comfortably full each evening. We thank God for a good number of folk that found the Saviour, some of them in full time service today.

In the town of St.Helier just outside the entrance to the Market Hall we were able to have a Christian Book Stall, run by a Christian literature evangelist, John Le Boutillier. At this time the Island had no Christian Bookshop and it was in desperate need of one. After the Crusade finished, some Jersey Christian business men found a butcher's shop for sale in the Market. It was bought and renovated, and the first Christian bookshop on the Island was launched. If you go to Jersey for your Summer Holiday one year, do pay the shop a visit – and buy a book!

But things changed by the end of the 70's

It was becoming increasingly clear that the era of this type of evangelism was rapidly coming to an end. Non-Christian people were missing from such crusades. This, seemed coupled with the fact that music, drama and even dance were beginning to play a big part in evangelism. However, I think that possibly the biggest problem was a growing lack of confidence in the gospel. This became evident when we were increasingly asked before missions, 'What else will we have in the programme besides the preaching?'

I remember being involved in a mission and asked to speak at a dinner for non- Christian men. There must have been 50-60 men brought by friends or work colleagues. The church said that we could not possibly expect the men to come for dinner just to hear a talk, and that they had booked a light jazz group to come and play before the meal. Afterwards, one of the guests I was sitting beside asked me 'why the jazz group.' Yes, it is my kind of music, but I wonder what it has to do with what I was told by my neighbour was to be a talk on, 'Is the Christian faith relevant today?'

Does this not reveal a lack of confidence in the message of the Gospel? I am sure that this was not the intention of the organisers, but it would seem to be the outcome of putting a 'sweetener' in before the message. Would the apostle Paul have put anything else in his evangelistic approach in the great cities of the Roman Empire on his missionary journeys? I cannot find any in the record of those journeys in the Acts of the Apostles.

I am sure that we have all heard of people being remarkably converted when there was apparently very little content as far as the message was concerned, and we rejoice that God works in spite of us all. But I am sure that if you are reading this book I don't have to emphasise that we ought to start and finish with Scripture and not with any pragmatic approach. For as Eric Wright says in his excellent book 'Tell the World.' No one engaged in the work of evangelism can afford the luxury of indifference to the norms of Scripture.' The words of the apostle Paul to the Corinthian church in 1 Cor.3:19 still stand. 'Each of you should be careful how he builds.'

We need to notice that the apostolic preaching had a breadth of content.It spanned the Old Testament as well as the new message of the gospel that was being delivered in and through these apostles. With pagan audiences Paul would often take his hearers back to the Old Testament message regarding creation, man's rebellion against God, but also that God had made a way for sinful man to approach a holy God and be reconciled to Him. These first Christian evangelists of the New Testament never thought of reducing or watering down the message of the gospel. They always sought to expose their hearers to as broad a content as possible. They were certainly aware that a right response to the gospel could only come that way. It was J. Packer who said that 'When evangelism is not fertilized, fed and controlled by theology, it becomes a stylised performance seeking its effect through manipulative skill rather than the power of vision and the force of truth.'

Make no mistake about it God was still in charge and master of ceremonies at the death of Jesus. He was not caught off guard, or sleeping. The cross was no accident. The Bible tells us that Jesus was 'the lamb slain before the foundation of the world.' This message of the cross is an integral part of the gospel and we must not lose our confidence in this gospel. At the cross God made an atonement for our sins in the death of His Son. So we can now offer Christ freely to the people and proclaim the cross with all of its limitations. For Jesus said, 'You are witnesses of these things.'

Peter in his great sermon on the Day of Pentecost said that 'This Jesus has God raised from the dead and He is Lord.' Men and women do not make Christ Lord, God has already done this for in the New Testament there was bowing at the beginning. The hymn puts it like this. 'He is Lord, He is Lord, He is risen from the dead and he is Lord.'

When the message about the birth of Jesus was announced to the shepherds of Bethlehem He is spoken of as 'Christ Jesus the Lord.' New Testament evangelists preached the Lordship of Christ. Paul in 2 Cor.4:5 says, 'for we do not preach ourselves, but Christ Jesus as Lord.' People coming to Christ in the New Testament came to him as Lord. In Col.2:6 Paul writes, 'just as you received Christ Jesus as Lord, continue to live in Him.' New Testament preachers preached His Lordship and sinners received Him as Lord. There is not one New Testament example of Christ being offered in any other way.

4

The Gospel in Greece

Paul the great New Testament Evangelist made inroads into the land of Greece on his first missionary journey. After leaving Philippi on being released from prison, Paul and Silas were then joined by Timothy and left for Thessalonica in northern Greece. After a short mission Paul was hounded out of this city by the Jewish extremists and was taken to Berea by some disciples. He did not stay long because the antagonists to the gospel followed him and agitating the crowds stirred them up. So the brothers in Berea sent Paul to the coast, but Silas and Timothy stayed in Berea. Paul bade them farewell, but urged Silas and Timothy to join him as soon as possible.

So here was Paul in Athens, the great intellectual and cultural centre of the world, and he was alone without the support of his two colleagues. No doubt as any one would do –he toured the city. But he was not swept off his feet by the majestic buildings or the splendour of the architecture. What gripped him was the idolatory – the city was full of idols. Seeing such a sight distressed him. Here was a blatant abuse of God's glory. Here was vivid evidence of the spiritual blindness of man's mind and reason.

Paul could wait no longer for Silas and Timothy to rejoin him. He could not swallow this scene of idolatory any longer. He began to reason and discuss the gospel with men everywhere and he proclaimed the gospel daily. Acts 16:17 says he went first of all to the Jewish synagogue, then to God fearing Greeks, and lastly in the market place day by day with those who happened to be there. He was zealous, full of fervour and passion, eagerly grasping every moment and opportunity. He knew that the stakes were high. The destiny of everyone he passed and saw, lay in the balance. They were all lost and doomed unless he could reach them with the gospel. Therefore no matter the cost, he had to do all that he could to reach them in their search for the truth.

So it was that the philosophers brought Paul to the Areopagus which is the Greek word for Mars Hill. It is not known whether Paul was asked to share the truth about God with a congregation of all the interested philosophers of the city, or before the official court. These people were aimless, empty and living meaningless lives. They had searched every philosophy and belief in the ancient world, and they had not found the one true and living God. They had searched and ended up empty for so long that they found meaning in life only by listening to new and novel ideas. In the words of Paul in Romans 1:21, 'Although they claimed to be wise, they became foolish.' So this was the audience that Paul found himself speaking to on Mars Hill in Athens.

Paul was unable to finish his message, because he was interrupted and the results were both tragic and wonderful. Some jeered, and in particular mocked the thought of the resurrection. Most of his hearers thought that life just finished at death. The idea that there was anything beyond the grave was completely beyond their understanding.

Others, a small minority, listening to Paul were more thoughtful, trying to grasp the message and to think through the implications for them as they understood the message. However, they were not ready for such a commitment. Listen to what the last verse of Acts 17 says, 'A few became followers of Paul and believed. Among them was a woman named Damaris, and a number of others.' When men and women heard the gospel in Athens as preached by Paul there were those whose response was ridiculous. Others said, 'not at the moment,' but thank God there were those whose hearts were melted by the gospel and whose response was that of the words Paul later wrote to the Roman Christians in Romans 10:9. 'If you confess with your mouth, Jesus is Lord and believe in your heart that God raised him from the dead, you will be saved.'

My arrival in Athens the capital of Greece was as a newly appointed evangelist for M.W.E. (Movement for World Evangelisation). For this trip I was joining my MWE colleague John Blanchard. We were met at the airport by the pastor of the Greek Evangelical Church. En-route from the airport to the church in the centre of Athens he told us that he hoped we had been informed that we were to preach for four nights on Paul's letter to the Phillipians!

John and myself, as you can imagine were taken aback by such news, for it was the first that we had heard of it. We arrived at the church nice and early-so shutting ourselves in the vestry we prayed fervently that God would help us as we decided who would take which section of this lovely epistle. The Lord greatly helped us, and it was a great lesson on the value of soaking yourself in the Word of God, so that when an emergency comes you can draw out from the great reservoir of gospel truth. I don't think that I will forget my first visit to Greece. This was also to be my first experience of having the message translated into another language. It was exciting to see the impact of the Word of God even through a translator.

The Athens pastor seemed to have a short memory concerning travel arrangements once we were in Greece. On one occasion we were booked to have an evangelistic rally in a neutral hall in Thessalonica. The film 'Jesus Christ Super star' was hitting town and we were to be the speakers on 'Who is the real Jesus?' Eric Clarke, another MWE colleague from Northern Ireland was going to sing at the rally. The Greek Orthodox Church was up in arms against this film and so it was going to be a good opportunity to preach the gospel.

Alas, the pastor had not booked us for a flight to Thessalonica on the day in question. We rushed to the railway station only to learn that there was not a train available that would get us there in time. So, as a last resort it was down to the bus station and yes there were seats available, and the bus would be leaving in about ten minutes. Our seats were right on the back row next to a Greek lady who was accompanied by three chickens in a basket! I remember saying to Eric Clarke, Paul never did it this way – he had to walk, or at best travel on a donkey or horse. Leaving Athens at about 7-30am we pulled into the Thessalonica bus station, about half an hour before the start of the meeting. It went well and we were thankful that we finally made it.

On another visit to Greece, we did have the programme and the intention was to preach the gospel in Athens and then go to Macedonia and to Katerini, where there is the largest Greek Evangelical Church in the country. There had been a time in this country when believers were severely persecuted. Many believers lived near to the church and even had some small shops nearby. In the church compound there was also an orphanage.

While we were in Athens I developed an abscess on a front tooth. With the pressurisation of the aircraft flying up to Thessalonica I was in a lot of pain and had a swollen front lip. I suggested to John Blanchard that I could not preach looking like this, but he said that as the Katerini folk had never seen me before they would think that I always looked like this! Instead he preached that night and I went to bed.

The next morning the Greek Pastor decided that I needed some dental treatment so took me off to the local Turkish dentist, escorted by the elders plus John. I was very reluctant to let the dentist loose in my mouth. He gave me an injection and lanced the abscess. It did relieve the pain, but returning home a few days later I had to have several teeth removed as the result of the Turkish dental treatment.

On another visit, the highlight for me was going out one night to a village in Macedonia. On arriving at the church with the pastor I noticed that he did not put the lights on in the church. As it grew darker the inside of the small building was only barely lit by the moonlight. I expressed some concern to the pastor who assured me that all would be well. I thought that maybe a fuse had gone and that somebody had gone to fetch an electrician. But nobody came and I was beginning to think that I might have to read my Bible and sermon notes by the light of the moon.

By this time I was standing outside the church door and looking across the fields. I noticed in the distance some small lights moving towards us. Then other lights could be seen, as one by one the folk carrying them stepped into the building until there was a wonderful glow. Each person brought there own light and I was provided with a lamp so that I could read and preach. I could not help reminding myself of the words of Jesus to his disciples. 'You are the light of the world.' We get so used to electricity in our homes and churches we can easily forget that Paul was a man who in every kind of situation preached the gospel.

Berea was a town and a church that fascinated me. They invited me to come and preach one evening. Unfortunately it was on a night when I was due in Katerini to preach. To my amazement they said that they would arrange a meeting at 5pm until 6pm. They would come and collect me by car and then bring me back in time for my 8pm meeting – so of course I said 'yes I will come.' The church in Berea was packed out which was remarkable as many of the congregation were shopkeepers from the many shops around the church. It would mean that they would close their shops for what in the town was a peak shopping time, and they would be losing money.

Dr Luke's record in Acts 17 of when Paul went to Berea after being chased out of Thessalonica, tells us in verse 11. 'Now the Bereans were of more noble character than the Thessalonians for they received the message with great eagerness and examined the Scriptures every day to see if what Paul said was true!' I had the same impression of them on the evening that I was privileged to be with them. Yes, they did get me back to Katerini just as the pastor was announcing the opening hymn.

Next on the agenda was a one week evangelistic mission with the Evangelical Church of Greece. Situated in Alexander Fleming Street the church was in a strategic position and I was very much looking forward to this week. The pastor of the church was also the medical director of St. Luke's Hospital, the finest independent hospital in Greece. I flew from London to Athens and then on to Thessalonica on a Friday with the mission starting on Saturday night. Dr. Demosthenes met me at the airport and apologised that the transport to St.Lukes where I would be staying for the week of mission was the hospital ambulance! After a meal we went down to the church for a pre-mission prayer meeting and to meet the church members, returning afterwards to my room – a ground floor small private ward.

Dr .Demosthenes said, 'I will call you in the morning and take you for breakfast.' By then, after my two flights and a fairly long prayer meeting I was ready for bed. I decided that I needed a shower before going to bed. Turning the shower on and stepping in I did not notice that it was on two levels. I managed to catch the instep of one of my feet and fell over. It was painful and not easy to get back to the bed. My first thought was to ring the doctor. Unfortunately although I had a phone in my room he had not given me the number of his flat which was on the third level of the hospital.

When the phone rang early the next morning it was the doctor telling me that he was coming down to take me to breakfast. I then told him my problem. 'Don't worry' he said, the x–ray department is just across the corridor from your ward. A nurse quickly came with a wheelchair and pushed me just a few yards across the corridor and the necessary x-ray was taken. After being treated, pain killers given and a walking stick provided, I was taken down that evening for the opening meeting. You can imagine what people said! Here, I was staying in the best hospital in the city, perfectly well on the Friday night and now with a foot bound minus one shoe and walking with a stick!

I received first class treatment every morning and by the time I was due to go home on the following Monday I was able to get a soft shoe on and dispense with the walking stick. That was not the end of the story during the week of Mission. During the day I was unable to leave my personal ward and the doctor was far too busy to take me anywhere, but it did give me time to read. However in the middle of the week the doctor said that he was taking the lunch time off and was going to take me, with his wife and children out for lunch. We were going down near the harbour to a very nice sea food restaurant. It was a lovely break from the hospital and I love sea food.

Returning to the hospital I was busy preparing for the evening meeting when the doctor phoned me to ask if I was okay. His wife had been violently sick and I assured him that I was well. Half an hour later he rang again. His two children were also sick and he was not feeling very well. I assured him that I was fine and we set off to take the evening meeting where he translated very well. In the middle of the night the bug hit me and this time I did have a buzzer to ring for the night nurse who came quickly.

Demosthenes came to take me for the breakfast that I could not face! His family were no better, but the gastro-enterologist was coming in that morning and would see me. He did, and diagnosed food poisoning. After some treatment, I was able to preach that evening! I have interesting memories of that week of the church in Alexander Fleming Street

The following year, I received an invitation to return to Greece and give the Bible Readings at the Pastor's Conference of the Greek Evangelical Church. After my previous experiences I was not too sure, but eventually said I would go. The week before the conference I stopped off in Athens and stayed with friends working with Arabs who were seeking asylum in Greece. They asked me to preach the gospel several evenings to this group. The husband of this couple was himself an Arab and so was able to translate into Arabic – another new experience.

From Athens, I was due to be taken up to Katerini by the pastor of the second evangelical church in Athens. While I was waiting for him to call and pick me up he came to tell me that he could not come. His wife had just received news of a close relative who had died and he would need to take her by car to the family home. 'Don't worry' he said, 'I have booked you on the express train, reserved a seat and somebody will meet you at the station in Katerini. It was a lovely day, and I was seeing Greece from another angle. After about 5 hours we were approaching my destination. I could see the city nestling in the foothills of Mount Olympus.

I picked up my suitcase and made for the door, only to discover that it was locked. Before I could reach the other side of the corridor, the train moved off! Some of the other passengers were really upset for me and one or two who spoke English said that the train was running a little late and that is why it stopped for only a couple of minutes. As you can imagine I was absolutely shattered. Then a man a few seats back asked me if he could help. He had a mobile phone and could call whoever was meeting me off the train, but because of the suddenness of the switch from car to train, I had not been given any name to contact. When I told him what the problem was, he asked me why I was going to Katerini. When I told him that I was going to speak at the Evangelical church he said, 'Praise the Lord, I am believer.' He then said , 'let me think for a minute or two' and then added , 'Please trust me, get off at the next small station and wait there and I will ring round some people.'

You can imagine my apprehension as the train pulled into a very small station. I jumped down and found just one bench near to a hut where the solitary station master was based. He waved the train away, en-route to Thessaonica. Half and hour later I could hear a phone ringing . A man came out of the hut, ushered me in and handed me the telephone. To my relief it was the pastor who should have met me. Evidently he was there, but he confirmed that the train had basically pulled in and pulled out again very quickly.

It was a relief that at last somebody now knew where I was, so I quickly asked him for his phone number and name in case there were any other problems! He told me to get a taxi, as every taxi driver would know Katerini.

Putting the phone down I went outside for a taxi, but there were none to be seen. I then tried to speak to the one and only station official and try to make him understand what I was looking for. Eventually after many drawings of a taxi, he seemed to understand what I wanted and made a phone call while I sat outside and waited. I thought that if it had been Paul then he would have got up and walked! But I was about 20 kilometres away from where I wanted to be, and I don't think that walking was on the agenda at that moment, particularly carrying a suitcase.

At last I could hear the sound of a diesel engine and a battered old yellow taxi drove up the road and stopped near to where I was sitting. With the odd Greek word and his even more odd English words, I eventually made him understand that I wanted to go to Katerini. I was never more pleased to at last arrive at my destination.

I thought, surely nothing else can possibly go wrong for me in this lovely land of Greece, and thankfully it didn't. At the end of the week I was to return to Athens by train. As they bade me farewell it was with the words, 'please get off the train at the Athens main station. If you miss that one then the next one is Piraeus, and if you miss that then you will be in the sea!'

Sitting in my comfortable seat on the Athens express I was reading again in my New Testament Acts 16 and 17 of Paul going to Thessalonica with the gospel and then to Berea, both of these cities for a limited time, and then down to Athens where he preached the gospel. God blessed his ministry and not only were churches founded in these Greek cities but the gospel is still preached there today and God had given me the privilege of seeing and sharing in this ministry 2000 years later. 'Have Bible –will travel,' and yes, the train did stop at Athens where a friend was waiting to meet me.

5

Return to Asia

Twenty years after being converted in Singapore, I returned to a very different city from the one where I spent two years during my National Service. This time it was to be just for the month of June with four weeks of evangelistic meetings all round the city. Singapore has nearly 3 million inhabitants and over half the population are under 21years of age. This age group is certainly reflected in church life and, as I was there during a holiday month, many students packed the meetings each night.

Tent Crusades have always been my great love, and so I was looking forward to this my first Tent Crusade in the Far East. I was not to be disappointed. The young people had worked hard in prayer and preparation. Nightly the low roofed, open sided, canvas cathedral was packed with young people. Serious minded students from the Colleges and University, student nurses from the General Hospital just across the road were well represented. The Tent was well lit and colourful and the amplification was efficient and loud- it needed to be, to compete with the roar of the Singapore traffic as it hurtled past on the main road just 20 yards from the Tent. They had asked me in advance for my sermon titles for each night. These were posted up outside the Tent in glowing neon lights. One evening, when I was speaking on the question 'Is God really a God of love?' the music from the film 'Love Story' was being played as the young people were coming in.

One evening I was highly amused when the opening hymn on the sheet was an old World War 2 Vera Lynn song 'You are my sunshine, my only sunshine.' I stood on the platform beside the song leader, an officer in the Singapore Army and tried not to smile as a I sang along, 'The other night dear when I lay sleeping, I dreamt that you were by my side.' But the nightly response to the gospel was wonderful as so many unconverted young people were present.

Each Crusade during the month was of 4 to 5 nights in different parts of the city and all organised by young people in their early twenties. There were early morning prayer meetings, and also others were praying in another hall while the gospel was being preached. All this commitment on the part of these Chinese young Christians was a great challenge to me, but also a further confirmation not only of the relevance of the gospel but its power to change the lives of people from all cultures and people groups.

From the oven like heat of the Tent Crusades, it was to the cool air conditioned luxury of the Hilton Hotel where I was to speak at the Annual Banquet of Singapore Youth for Christ. The problem for me was that I had not been warned that the Hotel was air conditioned! I had gone dressed in light slacks, a short sleeved shirt with a tie, whereas most of the guests were in dinner jackets, or shark skin suits. By the time I got up to preach I was freezing cold, and that was after 35 different dishes had appeared on the large circular tables that the guests were seated round. I felt and certainly looked as though I might have been a member of the cleaning staff, or a kitchen porter. After apologising for my dress sense, it was a lovely opportunity to share the gospel with some of the business men and women of this thriving economy. A very fine work is carried on by the Y.F.C in the city and over two thousand teenagers packed the National Theatre for their 15th Birthday Convention Rally.

It was while in Singapore that I had the joy of speaking and challenging young Chinese Christians to get involved in world mission. On their door step is the country of Indonesia with its population of millions. Over recent years, news has been trickingly through of revival in some parts of the country. I spent some time in conversation with an Indonesian Christian who was the superintendent of the Singapore Aquarium and he told me about this revival. Yes, the Bible and the message of the gospel can travel even to Indonesia.

Radio has for many years been a tool used of God to bring His Word to our world, and FEBA(Far East Broadcasting Association) had a studio here in Singapore. The director, Mr. Lauw Kin Guan, is an old friend. It was not only my privilege to visit the studios to see something of this strategic ministry, particularly in the beaming of the gospel to China, but also to record a programme for the Indian transmission. I little knew, that over the next 20 years or so, back here in England I would be involved with regular programmes for Radio Worldwide, United Christian Broadcasting and Good News Broadcasting. Radio has no barriers and today with the use of satellites it can reach the so called unreachables in most areas of the world.

Saints in strange places

There is always a sense of wonder when you see something of the grace of God in a man's life. This probably shows up most visibly in a prison situation. Changi prison brings back horrific memories to many older people, because it was here during World War Two, that the Japanese incarcerated thousands of British and Australian soldiers and civilians. If only walls could speak, what a story they would tell of hunger, privation, disease and even death – but what a different story now.

Today, the Singapore Government uses the prison for maximum security prisoners. Although the regime is spartan and the discipline firm, it is possibly one of the best run prisons in South East Asia. Certainly the authorities recognise the value of the gospel in the life of a man, and the Rev. Henry Khoo the chaplain, has a most fruitful ministry amongst the prisoners. I eagerly accepted his kind invitation to preach at three Sunday morning services.

Arriving a little late for the first service at 7am I could hear hymn singing wafting over the walls. They gave me a warm welcome and the service was led by the prisoners and not the chaplain. Before the prison choir sang (all of them convicted criminals) one of them gave a brief exposition of the first few verses of John 15. Thirty minutes was then given to me to preach the gospel and praise God that when I went back for the second Sunday morning, the chaplain told me that during that week he had led a number to Christ who had been convicted by the Holy Spirit of God during the message on my first visit. What a privilege to shake hands and speak with some of these men, quite rightly serving sentences for their crimes against society. Now, by the grace of God they are new creatures in Christ Jesus and brothers in Christ.

Singapore still has the death penalty for murder, and a group of gangsters were sentenced to death for killing three men in an armed robbery. During the months when their appeal against the death sentence was being heard, the chaplain had the joy of leading all seven of them to Christ. Their appeal against the death penalty was turned down and the day of their execution fixed.

Bible studies and prayer meetings became a daily occurrence and on the night before their execution, the chaplain slept in the jail so that he could be near them. For their last request they asked not for a banquet but for a loaf of bread and a bottle of wine! They wanted to remember the death of the Lord Jesus Christ for their sins, and who they would meet so soon. After praying with them, he led them in the singing of the hymn 'Jesus keep me near the cross' before they went one by one to the scaffold and into the presence of the Lord. None of them needed assistance to the gallows, but all walked steadily up the steps, and from the lips of each man came softly the hymn, 'Nearer my God to Thee, nearer to Thee.' – Such is the power of the gospel. The Biblical message of forgiveness in Jesus Christ is totally relevant even in a prison on the other side of the world.

The transformed lives of prisoners has had an effect upon some of the staff. The deputy governor had to be a witness at the judicial execution of a Tamil Indian prisoner. On the morning of his execution the condemned man was asked where he was going. He answered confidently, 'I am going to live with Jesus Christ who died on the cross for my sins.' That simple testimony by a simple man really shook the deputy governor, and he later told the chaplain that he had asked Christ to forgive and save him.

The third Sunday morning I left the chapel to the strains of the prisoners singing 'Amazing Grace, how sweet the sound that saved a wretch like me.' I just thanked God afresh for the wonder of His so great salvation, and for the privilege of yet again meeting saints in strange places.

Still in the area of Changi, but this time not in the prison, Mr Law Kim Guan, the local director of FEBA shared with me something of his concern for the thousands of Singaporeans, mainly young people, who frequented Changi Beach in the cool of the evenings and at weekends. I encouraged him to establish some form of coffee bar evangelism in order to reach them with the gospel.

It was a thrill on my return this time to see that the vision had been turned into a reality. 'The Life Saver's Inn' now operates week by week, not only serving coffee, but Mee Siam, Chicken Curry and Chinese Tit-bits. Thousands of young people have heard the gospel in this place and to date I was told that some 1,800 had been counselled.'Beach Rovers' as they are called, walk the beach with tracts and booklets, and engage in personal witness as well as inviting people into the Inn. Divine originality is one of the exciting things about Christian witness in this fascinating Island. It was a privilege to have had some small part in encouraging this venture, for in 1975 this was very different from anything outside the church.

There was one more mission in Singapore and that was in Bukit Panjang, and this was very different from the other opportunities. Meetings were held in the Chinese Methodist Church as it was strategically situated right opposite a night market. It was an ideal place to invite people in from the street. As always the church was packed with young people, but this time of a very mixed racial group, including Indians and even Malays It is forbidden to evangelize Malays because Malaysia is a Moslem State, but in Singapore there is no such law, although it is rare to see Malays in any Christian meeting.

Bukit Panjang is a strong Buddhist area and the powers of darkness and of occultisim were strong. Evil spirits were subjects upon which I had to answer many questions. One of which was, 'If I come to Christ will I have to give up ancestor worship ?'

From Singapore we drove up to Malaysia by car. It had not been easy to get a visa for this trip, but a top immigration official in Singapore suggested that I apply for a performance visa! I had planned to take a musical team of law students from the University who played different instruments and also a young Chinese singer named Robert Tan- and the visas were granted.

First stop was the town of Ipoh, and I felt at home here because the meetings (for Chinese young people) were in the YMCA theatre in 'Anderson Street.' Kuala Lumper was the next stop, driving north to where there was a big event happening in this capital city. Muhammad Ali was fighting our British Joe Bugner. The local paper featured a front page article on the big fight. Turning to the back page there was an article on the arrival of ' Dr.Peter Anderson and his musical Team of Love! '

Muhammad Ali was visiting the many Moslem schools during the day and so the Chinese schools invited Joe Bugner. He came from England so must be a Christian! He was no such thing, so you can guess what happened! Dr. Anderson and his Team of Love went to the Chinese schools. It was a great opportunity to preach the gospel in a positive way. Thousands of Chinese young people did hear the gospel during those few days in Kualar Lumper.

From K.L. we went still further north and over what was then a ferry to the beautiful Island of Penang. Although I was only there for four days of evangelistic meetings my programme included 7 meetings, one being in the Methodist girl's school with the whole school present -650 teenage girls.

We took the same route back to Singapore taking two days by car, and then had just a few days break before flying home. On my final day a dear Chinese business man invited me to lunch at a good restaurant in the city. The farewell lunch turned into a painful experience, when I swallowed a duck bone and had to be rushed to hospital for an emergency operation. This was not the end of the story. I was sharing a small room with another westerner and the nurse managed to take me down to theatre with his notes attached to my hospital gown. His name was Mr. Peterson and was due to have a stone removed from his kidney !- you can understand how the Chinese nurse was confused by the names. Fortunately the surgeon sorted out the mistake as the anaesthetist was late.

The offending bone was removed and several days later I was able to fly home feeling very weak, but thankful to the Lord for His hand of preservation in what could have been fatal.

6

Into Europe - Czechoslovakia

In August 1968, Audrey and I were in Jersey responsible for two weeks ministry at the Highlands Hotel. It was during the time of Alexander Dubcek, called by the citizens the 'Prague Spring.' He believed that communism should have a 'human face.' It was not to last long. One morning as we were dressing, we switched on our radio to hear the news that the Warsaw Pact Countries led by the Soviet Union had invaded Czechoslovakia. We knew nothing about the country at that time, except that it was part of the communist bloc. Little did we know that within a year we would be visiting the country for what was the beginning of a 25 year ministry with the Evangelical churches in this country at the heart of Europe.

My first trip was with John Blanchard my MWE colleague in the Spring of 1969, and during the next few years in this country there would be so many opportunities to preach the gospel and to teach the Word of God. We had met a wonderful Baptist Pastor named Milos Solc who took us round the country where in church after church people packed in night by night. At that time it was such a novelty and encouragement to have western preachers from Great Britain. It was a great harvest time for the kingdom of God, in a country where so many Christians had been imprisoned for the their faith, and many churches closed.

In January 1970, Eric Clarke another of our MWE colleagues joined us. This time however we planned to travel by road via Germany and then east into Poland and then down to Czechoslovakia- not the most sensible thing to do at this time of the year as we were later to discover. With the three of us taking turns at driving we made good time as far as Berlin. Security was tight at the border. Mirrors were put under the car and even a periscope into the petrol tank. We nearly had a disaster at the notorious CheckPoint Charlie crossing from Berlin into East Germany. There we realised that our car log book was registered in the name of 'Movement for Word Evangelism!' When the border guard asked for our car documents, John quickly handed him the car insurance leaflet, slipped the log book back into his briefcase and gave the guard a brochure describing the VW Fastback that we were driving. He turned over the pages and then gave it a very official looking stamp on the back page. . . . . and we were on our way.

Two hours later as we reached the East German/Polish border it began to snow. The Polish border guards and customs did not come out to see us – we were invited to go in and see them! To our surprise we were greeted politely and with interest as we were the only car crossing the border at that moment.

'Trans World Radio' had asked us to take some blank reel to reel recording tapes for the Polish Baptist Church in Warsaw. We had put them on the back seat of our car in an unsealed box so that it did not look suspicious. But when they asked us if we had anything to declare we said 'yes,' and then we were asked to bring the box in from the car and put all 50 recording tapes out on the customs table. The guards looked at them with some interest and talked amongst themselves for a few minutes, and then one of them who spoke English said, 'put them back in the box, go to your car and drive quickly because the boss comes back in five minutes!' How we rejoiced as we crossed the border and safely into Poland with 430 miles of driving ahead of us, through Poznan and then on to Warsaw. It was January, already the roads were packed with snow and ice and when 4pm came it began to snow again. Thankfully we did meet snow ploughs on the way, for the East Europeans know how to keep their roads clear, whereas in our country everything grinds to a halt if we get a few inches of snow.

We did have one or two hazardous moments. John managed to give us a magnificent slide and snake on one section of the road. I almost managed to decapitate a horse that was coming in the opposite direction pulling a small cart. Polish countryside in this area is very flat arable land and the snow blew horizontally across the road. Our car was driving well and the rear engine of the VW helped to give us traction. At one point we stopped to dig a Polish driver out of the snow when he had come off the road. How glad we were that we had several spades with us.

We made it to Warsaw at 11 pm and found our pre-booked hotel the Grand Orbis, but they could not let us have a room yet! The airport had been closed because of the bad weather and many people could not get out of the city. While we were waiting, they suggested that we had a meal in their restaurant. The meal was surprisingly good, but the service was really second rate for the top hotel in Warsaw. We tucked into our warm broth soup and duck with apple, followed by ice cream and coffee. While we ate our food, the small orchestra played and the local 'ladies of the night' plied their trade at the next table! At midnight we were finally given our room on the top floor where we eventually fell exhausted into our beds. It had been a very long day.

Looking out of the window early the next morning, we could see the city covered with a blanket of snow though it was not now snowing. After breakfast we re-packed the car which by now was frozen solid, but when we finally managed to open the doors the engine started first time. After fifteen minutes of scraping and spraying with anti-freeze, we looked at our street map of the city and set out to find the United Evangelical Church

Headquarters. It was difficult to get around the city unless we kept to the main road, but we had to go down some minor roads and managed to get stuck in the snow. A police van drew up behind us and some smiling police jumped out and helped to push our car out of the snow and we safely arrived at our destination.

In the 1950's a number of pastors had been imprisoned for their faith, but a strong Roman Catholic Church meant more freedom for evangelicals. During the really tough times for believers, Christians from all the denominations realised that they were one in Christ and so they were drawn together as never before.

From 1965 onwards, the studios of Polish Radio could be hired for recording Christian programmes and two a week could be transmitted. In those early years over 700 letters a month were received. The number of letters received is far greater today. Literature was offered to listeners, and the most requested book was 'Please send me the book entitled 'The New Testament.'

From the Evangelical Free Church we then were directed to the Baptist H.Q. and safely delivered the 50 recording tapes. There was great rejoicing when the Baptist Church Secretary saw them, because although they could hire the national radio studios for recording, they had to supply their own tapes. They were unobtainable in the shops, so our cargo was valued like gold dust. Tape recorders were needed for duplicating programmes and studio work. The British and Foreign Bible Society had a shop in Warsaw where they did have a limited supply of books and Bibles. Remember, this was still during the time when the country was governed by the communists.

One lady wrote in to the radio programme saying that she had a dream that someone knocked on the door and offered her a Bible. Another Roman Catholic lady wrote to ask for someone to come to her parish to preach this wonderful message, and adding that she had already spoken to her priest about it! Then one man wrote to say, 'Thank you for the nice singing, it can move even the worst heretic!'

After a quick cup of tea we returned to the United Free church to speak at their mid- week prayer meeting, at which about 70 people were present. John and myself preached and Eric sang, and then we were given a tour of the new church building seating 800 in the main auditorium. There were a number of other useful sized rooms including a guest room which we used that night, and also Bible school facilities, editorial and administrative offices. Students train for 5 years in the Bible Institute.

The next day we left for the long drive to Kracow. Snow and ice were our partners for the first part of our journey, but when we stopped for lunch the sun came out, and the road was much better for the last part of our journey. We arrived at the Hotel Cracovia at 4pm. After a hot bath and light refreshments we set out by foot to the main square, where we had been told that we would find the small United Free Church.

Eventually we saw a small notice indicating that a church was on the 3rd floor, number 15. There we were greeted by the small congregation with great joy, as we discovered that we were the first western Christians they had ever met during the days of communism. There was a lot of hugging and kissing, and we had a wonderful prayer time with them after the preaching. How we longed to have been able to give them some Christian literature, but we had none left.

Leaving the old town of Cracow early the next morning we managed to commit a traffic offence by turning left across the traffic. The police evidently whistled us to stop, but as we did not know what the whistle meant they chased after us. There was then the pantomime of them trying to make us understand what it was all about. Fortunately they were quite friendly, fined us about the equivalent of £5 and then allowed us to carry on! We then had yet another snowy journey to the Polish/Czech border. The border guards were again helpful and were for some reason fascinated by the spades that we were carrying in the car. Our cameras were noted on our visas but thankfully not the tape recorders that we were carrying. If they had been, then we could not have left them with the pastors, as when leaving the country later on we would have needed to show that the recorders were still with us.

We should have been heading for Prague and then the town of Liberec, but this was impossible in the weather conditions. We only made it as far as Brno where we decided to stay for the weekend. We booked into the Hotel Continental just across the road from the Evangelical Free Church. Sunday was a busy day when I preached at the Baptist church and John at the Church of the Czech Brethren. Eric 'rang the changes' and sang at both churches. We had lunch at a restaurant with Dr Jan Urban the pastor of the Free Church. He was subsequently to become the President of the Evangelical Churches during the communist days. That was a very tough job which called for great wisdom and courage.

Dr Urban and his wife became close friends and for 25 years Audrey and myself were invited to go to this lovely country and preach the gospel.

On our first meeting in the restaurant, Jan Urban gave us some very useful information about their church situation at that time. He told us that the Czech Evangelical Free Church had the Bible teachers, but the Baptists had the evangelists. What was encouraging was to hear how many people in high positions had been converted. For example he was rejoicing that a Professor from the University had walked into the church one Sunday evening when God met with him and he was saved. In his congregation Jan told us they now had engineers, seven doctors and one dentist!

They did have Bibles in the country and a few were allowed to be printed, but they were scarce. Of course Bibles were even more scarce in Russia. One of the Christian engineers had to travel to Russia on a regular basis and decided that he would try to take some in on his next journey. He set off with 45 Russian small print Bibles. As the train neared the Russian border he asked God for wisdom. When the train stopped at the last stop before the border, he got out and spoke with the driver who recognised him as being from the church in Brno. He took the Bibles, hiding them in the coal so that they safely arrived in the Soviet Union. 'Have Bible –will travel' in the coal tender at the rear of a railway engine – different from normal!

He then told us of a Christian man who had just been released from prison and who had been married a few weeks previously. A convicted murderer who had already served many years in jail had been put in his cell and very wonderfully been converted through the Christian prisoner's testimony. He was also out of prison and had to give his testimony at the wedding. They were expecting about 600 believers to be present for the wedding, but over a 1000 turned up!

From Brno we drove on to Pardubice then Vysoke and Sumperk, and once again the churches were packed out for the evangelistic meetings. On some nights there was standing room only. These were exciting days for the gospel in this country, and the novelty of having British preachers drew many who would not normally come to church. Night after night we witnessed the power of the Word of God as the Holy Spirit wrote it forcibly in the hearts of many people. A young doctor and his wife came to the Lord. The much prayed for brother of the Baptist pastor was converted, and many other folk both young and old repented of their sins and trusted in Christ.

Sumperk was an interesting town. Again it was snowing when we drove into the town square, where we managed to get stuck in a snow drift right outside the Russian Barracks. The sentry quickly came out, but he smiled as he saw our efforts to push the car out of the snow and back on the road.

The local Baptist pastor who had managed to visit the west on one occasion, said to me over tea one evening in this town, 'Why is it that in the west with so much opportunity that you do so little for the Lord Jesus Christ.' He also told us of a young English man teaching English in a factory, who went on a trip to Russia. Arriving in a small Russian town the Holy Spirit prompted him to ask a man in the street if there was a church in the town. 'I do not know,' he said. 'I have listened to a radio programme for three months and then I wrote for a copy of the Bible.' Now you have come into my street.Jesus must be alive.' Do you have my Bible ? Pulling a small print edition of the Russian Bible out of his pocket he gave it to the excited man.

The snow was now quite deep, but it was crisp and dry. In Sumperk we heard a remarkable story from the local pastor. Zatopek was a very famous Czech marathon runner and also a General in the Czech army. He was evidently converted in Mexico during the Olympic Games and said in his testimony that 'It is more important to meet Jesus Christ than to be a General in the Czech army.' Here in Sumperk we had the privilege of visiting an old folks' hospital and home. After meeting a dear old saint of 92 we were allowed to sing and preach the gospel on the hospital magnetaphone system.

Later we were taken to a pig farm where the manager told us that his wife had been in the meeting the night before and had talked about nothing else since coming home. We were royally ushered into their cottage and fed until we could eat no more. Very wonderfully they both came to the meeting that night and were converted.

In this town we had a remarkable experience. Before leaving we had to go to the local bank in the town square in order to change money. While we were in the queue, Milos Solc the Baptist pastor from Prague who was with us,spoke to the clerk behind the counter and said that Eric was a famous English singer who could sing in Czech and he would like to sing for us now! When Milos told us what he had said, we felt scared. The young lady behind the counter went upstairs to see the manager, who amazingly said 'yes.' As Eric stood at the Bank Counter and began to sing 'Burdens are Lifted at Calvary, Jesus is very near' the whole bank stopped work to listen, clapped and asked for an encore. Eric then sang, 'How Great Thou Art,' both of these songs in Czech. In the meantime John Blanchard and myself were beating a hasty retreat to the door thinking that at any minute now some of the garrison of Russian troops would come bursting in and arrest us ! Nothing of the sort happened. The audience clapped, some asked for autographs and then we were ushered upstairs for coffee with the manager. He then told us that one of his best workers in the bank was a Christian girl. What an experience ! I just could not imagine it happening in Barclays Bank on a Monday morning or any other day of the week.

On future visits Audrey was to accompany me as she was to have many opportunities to help and encourage the pastors wives and speak to young people.

With the Polish Churches in the country

Near to the Polish Border in Czechoslovakia there are a number of fine churches belonging to the church of the Czech Brethren. We had visited Velka Lhota, a small town when they were digging out the foundations of a new church. It was in a most beautiful part of the country with the backcloth of the mountains and the pine forests in winter flaked with snow. This place was also intended to be a conference centre —but no permission had been given during the dark days of communism, so the pastors and their families came here to have some rest and recreation.

On our journey here, a Polish/Czech pastor told us of his experiences when visiting Russia. He had found a way of delivering Russian Bibles by post via the post office in Brno. He said that over the past year he had been able to send 600 copies. They were taken by Post Office Vehicles. If some were stolen by the customs, he knew that they would be sold!

One day a Russian believer called to see him who looked as if he was a tramp. He was absolutely amazed by the Pastor's apartment in a flat over the church building, because there were so many beds. In fact a bed for every member of the household. In his home there was only one bed for himself, wife and five children! Pyjamas he had never seen, and when offered a banana, he started to eat it-skin as well! What a different world we live in.

The Pastor took us from Velka Lhota for another 15 kilometres over a snowy mountain road heading for Goldova. We were in his old VW Beetle and he would insist on talking to me and looking at me as he drove. Going round a bend the car skidded, shot across the road, hit a post that spun us back on the road like a top and finally crashed over the side of a ditch onto its side. The heavy snow drift cushioned our landing and we were safe. It really was a miracle that at that moment there were no vehicles coming the other way. I safely clambered out of one side of the car. The pastor and I had not even a bump. Audrey on the back seat had banged her head on the glass of the side window. I asked her to pass me my camera through the window without even asking if she was hurt! She has never let me live this down!

The pastor told us that he was very worried lest the police came along, for in his front boot were two boxes of Russian Bibles. If they had discovered them then we would have been in trouble.

Just at that moment a lorry came round a bend in the road. The driver asked if we wanted any help. A strong towing rope was unloaded from the lorry, attached to the VW Beetle and speedily pulled us out of the ditch. Mercifully, apart from a dent on one running board of the car it was undamaged and the engine started first time and we returned safely to Brno!

On our return to Prague we received an invitation from the Council of the Evangelical Free Church of Czechoslovakia to meet with them. They asked us many questions about the life of our churches in Great Britain. One senior pastor from Bratislava spoke of those in his church when he was in Presov, who had come to the Lord when we had evangelistic meetings there in 1971 and were now members of the church. It was such an encouragement to know that the Bible with its life transforming gospel had also made its mark in what was then still a communist country.

What probably challenged us most before we bade them farewell and left for home, was when one of the council said, 'We pray for your churches in Great Britain,' and when I thanked him and asked him why they prayed for us, he replied, 'Because you have the problem of freedom.' Here in Eastern Europe we feel that we have a responsibility to pray for you, that you will use the many opportunities you have to proclaim the gospel.' Many years later when freedom had come to this country and it had divided into two, the Czech and Slovak Republic, we again met the pastor, who had said 'we pray for you because you have the problem of freedom,' now said with a certain sadness,'Please pray for us because we now have the same problem.

Eleven months after the velvet revolution and the fall of communism

Having been in the country many times during the dark and difficult times, it was with a real sense of excitement that we looked forward to returning to the country under freedom. As always Audrey was coming with me and the Council of the Evangelical church had invited us to speak at a number of evangelistic missions. There was a lot of travel, from Karlovy Vary, the former Spa city of Carlsbad near the East German border, to Ostrava near the Polish border and then to Vsetin, a small town near to the Lower Tartra mountains.

In Vsetin the church had hired the local theatre for an evangelistic meeting. Posters were displayed in the streets and the young people had given out invitations in the town the previous weekend. On arrival we found a bookstall at the entrance to the theatre, with people flocking round it eager to buy a Bible or a Christian book. At starting time the theatre was full, about 400 people, and we were told that about a third of the audience were non-Christian guests who listened intently to the gospel. These were days of strategic importance in this country and it was imperative that the gospel reached the ears and hearts of the people before the false sects that were already coming into the country took over.

During the days of communism, Christians could only share the gospel in a church service in a registered building for religious purposes. Now they could move outside their own buildings and even do things in their own building that had never been done before. In Opava the pastor arranged a mission beginning with a dinner in the church hall in which believers could invite friends and neighbours. The format was very simple, eat a good meal provided by the church and then I was introduced to preach followed by questions. Apart from Sunday morning when we had a service in the church, all the other meetings were held in a local theatre and were well attended. After every meeting people stayed on to ask questions and talk about the Christian faith.Before the Saturday meeting the pastor introduced me to two young men.Nothing unusual in that,but it was unusual because they both had been allowed out of the local prison for the evening! The one who was going to share his testimony was inside for causing 'grievous bodily harm' but had been converted in prison.We discovered that since the 'Velvet Revolution' of 1989, the believers have open access to prisons and other corrective institutions.

During the later days of communism when we visited the town of Ostrava, Audrey and myself were invited to a special reception at the Town Hall with the deputy Mayor of the city.The communist secretary for religion in the city also invited us for lunch in a local hotel.When we arrived and were introduced to him we were escorted into a small private dining room, where on one side of the dining table was the Union Jack and on the other the Czech flag. He was most friendly and presented Audrey with flowers. Jan Urban, the church President told us later that when the man had some serious cancer surgery, the only person who visited him apart from his immediate family was the pastor of the church and not his communist colleagues!

So it was here in Ostrava now that freedom had come, that we had services in the newly built church. It had a beautiful auditorium for Sunday services but also had a café that served excellent food and was used for evangelism on a number of nights each week. Here in the church we were introduced to one of the elders who was just about to depart to Israel as the new Czech Ambassador.

Seventy miles south of Prague is the town of Pisek and here we found a newly formed Evangelical church that was really quite different from anything that we had seen so far in this country. It ran a second hand clothes shop in town, a printing press, a bookshop and a small orphanage. It was also in the process of renovating an old farmhouse that when completed would be a residential home for drug addicts. With a full time staff of 12, the church is also very much involved in evangelism and hires the lecture theatre of a local college on a Sunday morning. For my visit they had asked me to speak on 'The occult and spiritism,' and had placed posters and leaflets all over town. The theatre was packed out with people sitting and standing in the foyer and entrance hall. It was not only an opportunity to warn people about the dangers of the occult, but also to introduce them to God's supernatural experience in the gospel of the Lord Jesus Christ.

At the end of this visit, we were due to leave Brno by train for Prague. Jan Urban and his wife Libuse came to the station with us. We were aware that this could be our last visit to our greatly loved Czech Republic. As the train approached the station, we all felt that this might be the last time we would all together after more than 25 years of serving the Lord together in this country, so it was rather an emotional farewell.

But there was one last unexpected visit

Audrey was unable to come as she was unwell at the time, so this time I would be alone. During the days of communism, and now in the new era of freedom, we had been privileged to visit and preach in most of the Evangelical Free Churches. Dr. Jan Urban, now retired as their President had been a close friend for all of those years and for most of the time had been our main interpreter. He was a fine preacher himself, and an excellent translator. He as usual, arranged my itinerary for this final visit.

Arriving in Prague on October 5th, I preached at an evening meeting in the Zizkov church, where I was also able to screen the new Czech evangelistic film made by the Christian Television Association – and in the Czech language.

The next day I travelled by bus to Pilsen and then to Klatovy, near the German border where we held an evangelistic rally. One of those who came to Christ that night had been given a Gideon New Testament some months ago and had been reading it daily.

We returned to Pilsen the next day – a town famous for it's beer and the skoda car! The nightly attendances were not high, but there were always unconverted people brought by friends and some trusted the Saviour – all men.

I was asked on the Saturday afternoon to lead a seminar for the United Churches on evangelism, and on the Sunday afternoon to speak at a 'World Vision 'meeting and also to screen the Czech video film. It was a great joy to share this meeting with a missionary from Korea who was working in Pilsen. After a busy weekend I travelled by train back to Brno, the home of Jan Urban. The city has a large university and many students attended the church on Sunday. At a special meeting just for students they asked me to speak on the 'Victorious Christian Life,' and afterwards yet again there were many questions and a good discussion.

The next day we left by car for Olomouc where the Baptist Church had a Bible School. The Principal, who I had met on one of our previous visits, had 60 students in full time study. Surprisingly, it is also supported by the State for the training of social workers. The ministry of social affairs recognised that a moral and ethical training that is Christian orientated is an excellent training for social workers. The first two years of study are Biblically based, and the third year is for social sciences. I was invited to give a lecture on the gospel to the students, and the State paid me for it!

From Olomouc it was on the road again to Ostrava where we were joined by Jan Urban's grandson who was to be our driver for the remainder of my visit. Leaving the Czech Republic we drove across the border into Slovakia where my first meeting was in the village of Vavrisova near the foot of the beautiful High Tartra mountains. It was held in the oldest Baptist church in Slovakia. As we got out of the car we heard an announcement on the village loudspeakers of my subject for the evening. This was the first I knew about it!

After an early breakfast the next day, we had a short drive to where young people were having a house party and had asked me to bring them a message. The venue was a hotel owned by the Baptist church, confiscated by the communists, but now returned to the church under the law of restitution.

We continued our journey east to Michalovce, near the Ukraine border and the church that we had visited on two previous visits. There was as usual a good hearing for the Word of God and on the Sunday afternoon I repeated the 'World Vision' programme. It was sad to realise that during the dark days of communism the church had very little information as to what God was doing in the world and certainly could have no involvement in missionary service.

My visit was coming to its' end, but there was to be one final church - 80kms away at Presov, for an evening evangelistic meeting. It was a great encouragement to meet some of the folk converted in 1972, when Audrey and I had a series of evangelistic meetings in the town, and they were now serving the Lord in the recently built new church.

The journey home was long and tiring. A nine hour car journey from Presov to Brno, then four hours by train to Prague. My final night was spent on a bed in the kitchen, to be woken early when the lady of the house made her breakfast before leaving for work at 7am. A very tired but happy preacher flew back to England later that day.' Have Bible-will travel' had certainly been my experience once again during those last twelve days in the Czech and Slovak Republics.

7

Bulgaria - A Needy Country

Please do remember our brothers and sisters in Bulgaria,' was the plea of a Baptist pastor during one of our early visits to his country. 'We have problems ' he said, 'but the Bulgarian believers have bigger ones. During the next few months, I kept thinking about his request, particularly as he had given me the address of a church in Bourgas, a large city on the Black Sea coast of the country. He had also given me the name and address of some believers in that city.

Enquiries from different sources came up with the suggestion that I go as a tourist to the Black Sea. It was possible to book a holiday with a Government travel agency called 'Balkan Holidays.' Talking with my travel agent I discovered that I could fly from Gatwick direct to Bourgas, and then stay in a beach resort about 12 kms from the city. No visas were required as they came with the holiday booking.

I thought that a man on holiday alone might look suspicious. Our son was approaching his 15th birthday so I suggested that he should come with me, a suggestion with which he readily agreed- and off we went several months later.

As far as Bulgaria was concerned I really was an innocent abroad about custom's checks at the airport border. I had heard that next to Albania this was possibly the toughest communist country. We managed to obtain a few copies of John's gospel plus small print Bulgarian Bibles, plus Scripture Gift Mission Literature also in Bulgarian.

To our great delight there was absolutely no custom's control when we landed at Bourgas airport. The suitcases from the whole flight were unloaded and dumped in a great pile outside the main entrance to the airport. All we had to do was to pick them up and get on the coach that would take us to the beach resort that was called Sunny Beach! All of our Christian literature was safe. On subsequent visits to the country over the years that followed, there was still no customs control, and so we were able to take in thousands of copies of Christian booklets, and also much needed help in the way of recording equipment for the churches to use in their ministry.

We arrived on the Saturday, so thought that it would be good to go and look for the church on the Sunday morning. Loading our shoulder bags with literature we went by taxi into Bourgas to see if we could find the church. Alas, our first discovery was that the Czech pastor had spelt the name of the church in anglicised form and the people in this country used the Cyrillic script. All day Sunday we walked around looking for any building that vaguely resembled a church but to no avail. It would have been very dangerous to call into a Tourist information office and ask for details, so reluctantly we caught a taxi back to Sunny Beach.

We did have one more try on the Monday morning, but by then we realised that we had no chance of delivering the Christian literature that we had brought. However, my son John had an idea. Only a 15year old boy could have thought of this! He suggested that during the rest of the week we would visit as many public toilets as we could find, and leave behind either some SGM literature or a John's gospel, and this we did.

I did feel however at this point that distributing the Word of God in this way was not what I had really come to Bulgaria to do. Returning home at the end of the week it was with the thought that though I had tried to fulfil the wish of my Czech pastor friend it had not been possible. This was very disappointing to me.

Some months later, I received a message from a Greek pastor saying that if I went to the city of Varna, further up the Black Sea Coast from Bourgas, there I would find a small Baptist church, the only one left open by the communists in the city. He indicated.'It is easy to find because it is in a street named Georgi Dimitriov Street, just a few minutes walk from the city centre. That summer I set out again, this time on my own and flew from Gatwick to Varna. To my relief it was the same easy entry at the customs with all the luggage being dumped outside the main entrance to the airport.

The Greek pastor had also told me that in the church there was one man who spoke English whose name was Geliasko Geliaskov. Leaving the airport en-route to the holiday resort of Golden Sands, the travel guide was giving us a run down on the wonderful economy, information that none of us wanted at nearly midnight! Very wonderfully, driving through the city centre she pointed out a statue and said, 'Over there is a statue of Georgi Dimitrov one of our heroes.' I quickly made a mental note of the location in relation to other buildings, and thanked the Lord in my heart that He had provided a guide to point out the very road that I needed to find.

It was well after midnight before our coach pulled into the resort which was about 12kms north of Varna. Falling tired into bed and with my alarm clock set for 7am, I was up and out of the Hotel heading up to the main road to wait for a bus into the city. It was very amazing that the bus actually stopped near to the statue of Georgi Dimotrov and street named after him.

I walked up and down looking for what might be a church, but to no avail. Then I noticed some people going through a door in the wall, and then a few minutes later some more. When yet again a few people opened the door, I felt that this was the church. On opening the door, I found myself in a courtyard, at the end of which was a small building – the church.

Walking up the few steps into the building, I found a seat on one of the wooden pews and an elderly man came and sat beside me. He shook my hand, welcomed me to the church in English and told me his name. It was Geliasko Geliaskov, the very man that I had been told to contact. That was the beginning of a warm fellowship with him and his family for a number of years during the Communist days.

Returning to the resort I made sure that I spent the rest of the morning on the beach, so that if I was being watched by the authorities they would at least see me doing what other tourists were doing. Usually, I would go to town on the local bus but there was a small boat that went down the coast to Varna harbour, and this made a pleasant change from the battered old bus.

Pastor Gospodinov made me very welcome, and on a Sunday morning would ask me to bring greetings to the congregation. This was an East European practice and I was delighted to do this. I was not allowed to stand in the pulpit as that would have been preaching, but with my translator Geliasko, and standing at ground level below the pulpit I could give my greetings from Paul, and spend twenty minutes doing so. I commented that Paul had a lot to say when he wrote from Rome!

The same would happen in the evening service, when I might switch and bring greetings from Peter, Timothy or even Matthew, and this was the pattern for a number of years. It was however, a courageous thing for the pastor to do inviting me to speak, particularly as the State security police might have an informer in the congregation. One Sunday morning the pastor introduced me to a man that I did not recognise, as being one of our 'fine Bulgarian policemen,' much to the man's embarrassment!

There were a number of highlights during those dark days in Bulgaria. The first was when Audrey and myself were able to take 35 members of the London Emmanuel Choir, with Muriel Shepherd the conductor, to Bulgaria. They booked with different travel agents for the same trip and hotel, and for the same week. It was a nightmare getting the choir from the holiday resort down to the church, so the plan was to send them off in three and fours on the local buses over several hours. Those that arrived at the church first had time for fellowship with the believers and then that group were the first to leave after the service. The last group to reach the church were then the last to leave after the service. We had also arranged that choir members would take either Christian literature in the Bulgarian language or a number of cassette recorders for recording services and also portable radios that had short wave on them so that they could listen to the programmes in Bulgarian broadcast by Trans Word Radio. Audrey and I seemed to spend the week during the day delivering these valuable gifts to different locations.

Bulgarians love choral music, and the members of the London Emmanuel Choir had actually managed to learn a good number of their choir pieces in the Bulgarian language. The Bulgarian believers were astonished to hear the choir sing in their language. 'Bravo, bravo!' was heard all round the little church. On the last night the choir left their music books on the chair as a gift to the Bulgarian choir

Another highlight was to get 'Read, Mark, Learn,' a booklet of Bible readings by John Blanchard into Bulgarian. Getting it translated accurately was difficult and I looked for a professional translation agency in England, but was unable to find anyone who could work with the Bulgarian language. One Sunday, I was talking with one of my friends in my home church about the problem. He said that he was doing some insurance for a translation agency just outside the city of Leicester. As I did not want to personally ask them, he said that he would. A few days later he rang me to say that yes, they did have a very good Bulgarian translator who worked part time for the BBC. And would be willing to do this. If I remember rightly, it only cost £500 which was a bargain.

When I took the first photo copy of the manuscript into the country, I was told that it was an excellent translation. When I told them that the name of the man who had translated it was Georgi Markov, they said that he had been a well known Bulgarian playright who had come from an Orthodox background, so had a sensitivity towards the Scriptures. God certainly made sure that his Word was translated accurately.

Having it printed was the next step, and this we did giving the copies a plain white cover and small print so that we could keep the book as small as possible. Three thousand copies were printed, and over the next few years with the help of others visiting the country we were able to get all the copies into the hands of believers. We had just thought about getting a second book translated, when one day there was bad news on our television news programme. It was that our translator had been murdered by the KJB. One of their operatives had pushed the spike of an umbrella into his leg on London Bridge and the tip had poison on it and he died!

During those days, although I did preach in the church, some of the most valuable time was spent in the homes of believers. Fellowship with them was very precious and they always served us with food that they really could ill afford. I remember on one occasion being sat down at a small table and served a large helping of roasted chicken while the rest of the family sat around the room and watched!

I meet some very special people...

It was just beginning to get dark when I arrived at the church one evening. Pushing down the handle on the outside of the gate, it creaked open and I was safely inside the courtyard. Although nearly an hour before the service some had gathered for fellowship, and we sat on wooden benches under the vines and greeted each other in the name of the Lord Jesus.

Word had been sent to the pastor of my arrival, and soon he came hurrying out from his small house attached to the back of the church. His face as always was creased in a smile. When the service began it was simple and direct and unlike many other parts of Eastern Europe, it only lasted for one hour.

There were not many preachers amongst the few pastors left in the country and the ministry is mainly of an exhortational kind. At the moment the pastor of this church is preaching his way through some Bible Study outlines that I had brought him on a previous visit. My sermon notes always had to be handed over, translated into Bulgarian and then preached in another part of the country.

At the end of the service a special meeting for members only is announced, and I am invited to remain. It is to consider the acceptance of a lady for baptism and then into the church fellowship. Standing at the front of the church she was grilled about her faith. How did she become a Christian ? It was lovely to hear that it was through reading the Bible in January of that year. Why did she want to be baptized and join this local church ? What about her unconverted husband ? Would he stop her coming to the church ? If she was persecuted for her faith, what would she do ? Her answers must have satisfied them all because the matter was then put to the vote and she was accepted with great joy. I could not help but wonder what would happen if acceptance into membership of some of our churches was done on the same lines!

Having been accepted by the membership, she was now to be baptized. Unfortunately the baptistery in the church had sprung a leak and would not hold water, so the good lady was to be baptized in a lake outside the city. Everyone quickly left the church and by various routes made their way to the lake. By now it was dark and chilly, notwithstanding this the pastor and the lady went down into the lake and she was baptized upon confession of her faith in the Lord Jesus Christ.

They that honour me I will honour

Maria had been born into a believing family, and early on in her teenage years she had come to personal faith and trust in the Lord Jesus Christ. Studying hard at school she had qualified in economics and book keeping, and on leaving school became a clerk at a local State enterprise factory. Being an easy talker and somewhat of an extrovert, it was not long before all in the factory office knew of her Christian faith. Each lunch time she would take her New Testament from her pocket and show it to many who had never seen a copy of any part of the Bible before.

One day she was summoned to the Director's office and warned about the dangers of believing in God.'This fanaticism must stop' was the order.'If you don't stop this stupid talk about Christ, and if you don't stop attending the church then you will lose your job.'

Maria continued with her cheerful witness and her attendance at the evangelical church. Not many more weeks passed before she was once again summoned to appear in the Director's office and this time it was to be asked the question.'if you have a choice to go to church or hang, what would be your decision ?' Her reply was immediate,'I will hang for Jesus.''You are too stupid for words,' shouted the Director.'You are sacked —leave this office and this factory immediately.'

Maria went home that night wondering just what she should do, but one thing she was sure of. She would never stop telling people about her Lord Jesus Christ. Before going to bed that night she turned to her well thumbed New Testament and read the familiar words of Jesus in the Gospel of Matthew.'Seek first the kingdom of God and His righteousness, and all these things will be added unto you.' Yes, she could sleep content with the assurance of that promise from her Lord.

Within three days of losing her job, she received a letter saying that she was to report for work at another enterprise nearer to her home and therefore far more convenient for her.

Arriving at the new office she was called to the Managing Director's office. Greeting her kindly he said,'I understand that you are a believer. It is not important to me that you do or do not believe – what is important is that you work hard.' Maria as always worked hard and soon was promoted to private secretary to the Managing Director and even had opportunities to share her faith with him. One morning when the mail arrived, there was a batch of letters marked confidential. She did not open them at first, but took them straight away to her boss.' You may open all my mail,' was his quick reply,'for I trust you more than I do my fellow communists.'

Saints in strange places

The storm clouds were gathering over the city as the ancient bus, packed with its cargo of people tightly packed in,most of them standing, headed for the town centre. Before we reached the terminus, lightning was flashing across the darkening sky and thunder reverberated from the nearby hills on the outskirts of the city.

Jumping off the bus I raced through torrential rain into the nearby Orthodox Cathedral. Other rain avoiders rather than worshippers, were crowding in and the local priest with an eye to business was trying in vain to sell a few candles. There was little artificial light in the building and few chairs. Elderly people were lighting candles in front of various icons and the atmosphere was heavy with the smell of incense. Tourists were quietly wandering around and looking up at the great doomed roof with its marvellous painting of the last supper.

It was obviously time for evening prayer, because a priest appeared from behind a curtain at the back of the church and standing by a lecturn began to sing the liturgy in a beautiful tenor voice. The elderly continued with their prayers and candles, while the tourists carried on gazing and trying to shoot pictures until another priest indicated to them that taking pictures in the Cathedral was forbidden.

The rain now ceased as quickly as it had started and saw the hasty departure of those sheltering from the downpour. An assistant priest arriving late, came in hurrying. Depositing his dripping wet hat on the front seat he opened another service book and just made it to pick up the bass part of the liturgy. The sad thing was to discover later that although the Orthodox liturgy is full of Scripture, most of it is in 'Old Bulgarian' and the people could not understand it. They had the word of God, but not in a way they could understand.

I stepped out of the Cathedral and following the plan that had been given to me, I set off through the city to a house meeting. I found the apartment without difficulty, rang the bell and was quickly invited in. Coffee was served, needed medicines and literature handed over. Then as always I was asked to share a spiritual message from the Bible. About a dozen young people had gathered in the house for this special occasion and they listened so intently to every word. All of them had a Bible or a New Testament and they eagerly turned to every reference quoted and then translated into Bulgarian.

After the study came the questions, and for the next two hours it was question after question.'How can I witness for Jesus in our country ?'What do we say to atheists about God's existence?' In my job I am forbidden to attend church, what should I do? In the factory, if they know that I am a Christian I will not get promoted.'

By now it is late and I have to leave otherwise I will miss my bus back to the holiday resort. I quietly slip out and down the stairs and just make it to the last bus. It is almost empty – and for the last few kilometres I am the only passenger.

Through many years God has allowed me the privilege of ministry in many parts of the world in some exciting and thrilling locations.Possibly this meeting in a flat on the seventh floor of a block of flats with twelve young dedicated young people wanting to be the best for God in their country, was one of my most memorable.

What does your faith cost you ?

It was a miracle that Vasilov had been allowed to study at University in Bulgaria. Most believers were usually excluded from higher education as being 'politically unreliable.'

His father however had been a great patriot and fighter during the days of the revolution, and for his father's sake and also the fact that Vasilov was a brilliant student, he was allowed to go and study. The political Director at the University warned him that there must now be an end to all this Christianity nonsense now that he was going to study to serve the people.

Vasilov was not afraid to let it be known that he was a believer, and the first Sunday morning at University he found his way to an evangelical Baptist church in the city. The following Sunday morning, a State photographer with plain clothes police arrived and started photographing the congregation. Vasilov refused to hide his face, even though some believers got up and quickly left the church. His photograph, suitably captioned, then appeared on the University notice board after which he became the laughing stock of his fellow students. Valuable text books began to disappear. Work handed in for marking was never returned, but he finally passed his examination with flying colours. He had proved as countless thousands before have proved. 'They that honour me, I will honour.'

Returning to his home city to commence his career he was met with 'sorry, no job for you' wherever he tried to find employment. By now he had married his childhood sweetheart and a baby was on the way. He desperately needed a home and work, for the young family were still living in his parent's home. Then came a directive from the authorities that because he was a parasite on the socialist society he must go and serve in a labour camp for two years. They did say however to him that if he would turn from this Christian superstition, life would be different and work could be found for him. He hesitated for a few days and this was not an easy decision to make. Denying his Lord Jesus was impossible, and so to the labour camp he went – for two years!

Taking help

For a few days before every trip my stomach would turn over and sleep did not come easily. There were many things that I would have liked to take but flying limits the weight that you can take. Money is the easiest, as the country needed western currency and there is no restriction on the amount that you can take with you. Special medicines were bought, plus spare bulbs for projectors. Vitamin tablets, music books, a few Bibles and Scripture Gift Mission booklets are always packed into the suitcase. When I leave for the airport I hope and pray that they will not want to weigh my hand grip – and it is a relief when they don't- for all the heavy stuff is in it.

As always the Russian jet is late in leaving, but makes up for lost time on the journey. There were no frills on this plane. Even the stewards didn't appear until one hour after take off, and then frantically served a cold salad followed by coffee, beer, or lemonade!

Three and a half hours later the plane landed. As usual coming through border control presented no problem. I am still amazed how easy it was during those dark days of Communism to bring in priceless Christian literature. It was always a long wait outside the airport for the coach to take me to my hotel, and then only a few hours sleep before getting on the local bus back down to Varna and the church for the Sunday morning service.

I doubt if there were more than a hundred people present this morning. Most of the congregation I recognised from previous visits and many of them dear friends now. The pastor as usual invited me to bring greetings, and later in the week there will be an opportunity for me to preach on three evenings. At the conclusion of the service many believers come to invite me to their homes to share a meal and fellowship with them. They have little of this world's goods compared to us, yet they have discovered in a wonderful way the joy of fulfilling the Scriptural exhortation about being 'given to hospitality.' Yes it is dangerous for them to be friendly with visiting westerners. The pastor had only recently been called to the police station to explain why he had allowed westerners to bring greetings in his church.

News in the country was not very encouraging. One pastor who had baptized two young men in the river had been ordered to leave the town. Some of the more courageous men had spoken out about this injustice, and now they were working in a labour camp at the end of the country. Two of the older pastors, I was told, had died that month, and there were no younger men being allowed to take their place. In spite of this, God has been working and the ones and twos have come to Christ and others are seeking and asking questions. Remarkably, the believers are not downhearted, but they were battered and bruised and they pleaded with me to ask believers in our free country to pray for them.

Farewell

It was my last night at the church on this trip. With God's help I had been able to preach four times in the one and only registered church in Varna. My messages for those nights were from 1 Peter under the title, 'You are the people of God.' I had spent many hours with my interpreter before each service. I had to write my notes out for him in large print because due to diabetes he was slowly losing his sight, but God enabled us both in the preaching. Attendances grew each evening and the authorities obviously aware of what was happening had done nothing to hinder. As the pastor said on the last night in his quaint English translation, 'The Ghost that is Holy was protecting you.'

As the final service drew to a close the congregation stood and sang with much feeling and warmth that lovely old hymn, 'God be with you till we meet again,' although when I recognised the tune and asked my interpreter what the words were, he translated them to me as 'God be with you, see you later.'

Leaving the church and walking slowly down the dark, tree lined road towards the city bus station I recalled the events of the past two weeks. Apart from the four nights in the church there had been a house meeting in some part of the city every other night. One had been constantly reminded of the pressure that these people operated under.' Please don't speak any English as we walk up the stairs of the apartment block' was the quiet request

Being picked up by car one evening, we drove past two policemen standing on the street corner and I noticed that my kind host the driver went very tense.Later on I discovered that it was not permitted to give westerners a lift in your car.

Another evening going to a house that I knew well and could have walked there in five minutes – I was taken on two buses to get there.Over the next hour people arrived in two and threes. The curtains were drawn as soon as it was necessary to switch on the lights, and the Bible study started.Most of the believers had some copy of the Bible or New Testament, and all of them looked well used and many were in need of replacing, but the communists would not allow any to be printed, so all copies had to be carefully brought in from the west.

I met one dear man who had been released from prison having served two years for holding a meeting in his home for those who wanted to study the Bible. Then there was an exciting evening when most of the church members went to a concert being given in the town by one of the believers daughters. Music was one of the few professions along with sport in which believers could get to the top.Scattered around the audience were folk from the church and at the end of the recital they flung bouquets of flowers at her, the local paper reported a very successful debut!

There were so many things that tumbled over in my mind on that final night as I reached the bus station. Early the next morning as I returned to the airport and the plane that would wing me back to freedom I just thanked the Lord in my heart that I had been privileged to meet and serve my brothers and sisters in Bulgaria – and I thanked the Lord that they had certainly ministered to me.

The end of an era

On my next trip to Bulgaria Audrey was coming with me. Getting off the plane at Varna Airport and into immigration we found ourselves called away into a side room where we were put under arrest. It was something that I had often thought about although not with any fear, and now it had happened. Our suitcases were rescued outside the main entrance and we had to unlock them while they went meticulously through every item in the cases. They even took away and unstitched the shoulder epaulets of my jumper to see if anything was stored away secretly.

It was amazing that for this trip I had decided to take no Bulgarian Christian Literature and only had with me my English New Testament and sermon notes in English. Two plain clothes officers searched us and questioned us in Bulgarian that was then translated to us in English by a uniformed officer who was with us. In our luggage they found a street map of the city and looked at it very carefully to see if any street or house was marked. It wasn't!

Why did I go to the Baptist church they asked me, and not to the beach. I could honestly tell them that I was on the beach every morning and that in the evening if I been a gambler I would have gone to the casino. However as I was a Christian I would go to the church. All of this conversation went on for several hours. The plain clothes officers left the room periodically, leaving us in the care of the uniformed officer. He spoke reasonable English, and Audrey engaged him in conversation asking him about his family, and then showing him pictures of our children. He then brought her a glass of water when she said that she was thirsty, but he didn't ask me if I would like one!

When the others returned it was obvious that they were not happy because they had not found anything on us is that they could call illegal. They did insist however that I had broken the law the previous year. When I asked them what the law was, the only answer I received was 'You know!' Then we were told that we were to be deported and never allowed back again in their country. To our amazement they then told us that we were going to be deported to Helsinki in Finland, despite our protestations that if they were going to deport us then it must be back to our own country. All of this was to no avail, although they did say at this point that Audrey could stay!

We were taken by a police van to where a Russian plane was waiting to take off. We were escorted on carrying our own luggage up the steps and into the aircraft. As you can imagine we were looked at with some suspicion by other passengers on board. As the plane took off, my thoughts were first of all for my Bulgarian brothers and sisters who had been expecting us to be with them again at the church. My passport had been stamped 'deported' and so I knew then that it would not be possible to return to the country again.

As the plane neared Helsinki we began to wonder if we needed a visa to visit the country of Finland. As we walked across the tarmac, we were the only passengers carrying their own luggage. As we joined the queue at immigration- something remarkable happened. A well dressed man came up to us, squeezed my arm and said to me in English, 'you are welcome in our country.' – and sure enough we were.

Ours was evidently the last flight of the day and the airport was beginning to close down. We needed a bed for the night. Audrey noticed that a littler kiosk was still open. So while I sat on the luggage she managed to communicate our need to the lady in charge. She then telephoned the nearby airport hotel who said that they would send their mini-bus to pick us up, which much to our relief they did.

In those days when you visited Bulgaria as a tourist you had to pay not only air flight in advance, but also hotel accommodation and food so you didn't need to take much in the way of extra money with you. Counting up the money we did have, we found that we had $100, which in those days was a lot of money in Eastern Europe- and the room with breakfast was $65!

This was the first time I had taken a credit card with me to Bulgaria so felt sure that I could at least buy an air ticket for us to get back to London. The hotel receptionist kindly telephoned Finnish Airways to see if they had two seats-` to London for the next morning and they confirmed that they had and I could pay by credit card.

Arriving back at the airport the next morning, I went to the ticket desk and asked for the tickets reserved in my name and signed the necessary credit card document, taking them back to Audrey and saying 'we are on the way.'Then I looked at the boarding cards and credit slip. At that point I had not worked out the value of Finnish currency with relation to sterling. I discovered that I had bought Business class tickets! Under pressure on arrival at the hotel I had only asked if there were two seats to London, but had not stated 'economy class.'When we did get on the plane I walked back into economy class and there were no spare seats. So the Lord took us back to England in great comfort, even though it was an expensive way to go.

We had left Gatwick early on Saturday morning to fly to Varna. In the evening we were deported to Helsinki, and then on the Sunday morning took a flight back to London. It did strike me just how strange it was that the communists were so frightened of the Bible that they had to go to such lengths to stop me taking this great message of the gospel into their country.

The following week some friends contacted me to say that they were going on holiday to Bulgaria and was there anything they could do to help the church. I quickly rang them to ask if they would visit the church to tell them what had happened. This they agreed to do. It is wonderful how God always has people in the right place and at the right time.

On returning home from their holiday, they rang to say that some of my friends had been taken in by the secret police and asked questions about me. Evidently the police thought I was responsible for all of the Bulgarian Bibles smuggled into the country over the past six years! Another believer was told that I was the President of the Baptist Union! Later on I discovered that the one and only believer who had a car had been summoned to the secret police headquarters and asked if he knew me. He evidently said no, he didn't.They then produced a photograph of me getting out of his car. Several years later when I met this brother again and asked him about lying to the police, his reply was 'Is it wrong to lie to the Devil?' I am not sure about this answer, but then I had never been put in the position. I might have done the same.

For the next three years

Shortly after our arrest and deportation to Helsinki, the one remaining Baptist church on the city of Varna was destroyed. Bulldozed to the ground by the authorities to make way for flats. However they were allowed a plot of land on the outskirts of the city but getting to it was difficult. There was a long pathway from the main road that was terribly difficult to walk up in winter. Believers first of all met in the open air to sing and pray as they started slowly to build a new church. German believers gave them an old bus, so that they could pick up the old people from the town and bring them to church. A small basement hall was completed first and meetings commenced here. Work up stairs in the main hall went slowly on. News trickled through to me and I was praying that the Iron Curtain would collapse and that it would be possible to take up the Bulgarian ministry again.

When it all happened it was so quick and spread like wildfire all over Europe. At this time we were visiting our daughter and family who were working as missionaries in the Phillippines with O.M.F. Our son was on the phone from London, to say that the Iron Curtain had collapsed and that freedom had come. You can imagine our great joy that God had stepped into the situation and on our return to England three weeks later I quickly set off to the nearest travel agency to see when I could book tickets for my beloved church in Bulgaria.

8

Freedom Spreads to Bulgaria

In the years 815 and 827 two brothers, Methodius and Cyril were born in Thessalonica in Northern Greece. Both became priests and shared the same holy desire to spread the gospel. So they became missionaries to the Slavic nations of Moravia, Bohemia and Bulgaria. How did this come about ? In 862, just seven years before the death of Cyril, the prince of Moravia asked for missionaries to be sent to his country to bring the good news of Christ. He added one more request, that the missionaries should be able to speak the language of the people.

The two brothers volunteered and were accepted. In doing this they realized that they were being asked to leave their own country, language and culture out of love for Jesus. This they did willingly, and together they invented a Slav alphabet and then translated the Bible into the Slav language.

Some in the church at that time did not approve of the Bible being translated into a native language, so it was not surprising that the two brothers faced criticism. They were called to Rome to have a meeting with the Pope, and quite remarkably Pope Adrian the Second showed his gratitude and admiration for the two missionaries. He approved their methods of spreading the faith and named them Bishops. It seems that Cyril, died before he could be consecrated a Bishop, but Methodius on the death of his brother returned to the Slav countries and continued his gospel labours for another 15 years until he died on April 6th, 885. Although the alphabet they produced was not, as thought, the Cryillic of today; it was the foundation for the translation of books of the Bible to develop a Slavonic Script.

There is no dispute but that these two missionaries were used of God to lay a foundation for people to be able to read the Word of God for themselves.

On the anniversary of the death of Cyril, after the collapse of communism the Orthodox Church in Bulgaria had special celebrations. The Jesus film had recently been translated into the Bulgarian language, and the secretary of the project asked the secular cinema to screen the film as a tribute to Cyril. It was Cyril who first made the gospel record of the life of Christ available in a language that they could understand. So for example, in the city of Varna on the Black Sea Coast, six of the major cinemas in the city screened the film as the main event for a whole week. Thousands of Bulgarians attended every night and we will never know how many were actually confronted for the first time in their lives with the life of Christ as contained in the Gospel of Luke.

Throughout the city there were posters and display panels publicising the film and the mayor of one small outlying town actually put the film on in his town hall.

Back to Varna

So, I was returning to Varna for the first time since the collapse of communism. The Bible certainly had been unconquerable during the dark days of darkness and oppression, and on the plane across Europe and when landing at Varna I must confess to having a sinking feeling in my stomach when going through passport control. It seemed to sink even further, when the officer having put my passport into the computer, picked it up and went through a door into his checking post. Thankfully he soon came back with the assurance that I was very welcome.

I was up very early on the Sunday morning because I needed to be picked up and taken to the outskirts of the city to the Baptist church that was being built. It was up the muddy path that I had been told about, and then there was a glorious reunion with many of my old friends from the demolished church in the city centre.

Those days after the fall of the old regime were wonderful days for the gospel. Most citizens had never had the opportunity to hear God's Word, and there was a certain curiosity to at least go to a church for the first time, and hear what is was that the communist for so long said was all a fable and totally untrue.

As the church was still being built, all the meetings were held in the lower hall that seated about 100 when full. It was not easy for believers to get to this new church because if you lived down town it meant two bus rides.

The day before the series of meetings was to start, the city bus company went on strike. There was little petrol available for private motoring. In any case very few believers had cars. The path to the church was muddy and waterlogged owing to the unusual heavy rainfall. It looked as though it was going to be a disaster as far as the meetings were concerned. However, the bus company said that it would break the strike as far as the church was concerned and hire us a bus for each evening. We drove round the city picking up people for the meetings, while others made their way to the church and we were full each evening. We had planned that the meetings would be Bible teaching for Christians. Many Christians certainly came, but they also brought unconverted friends with them, many of then carrying copies of John Blanchard's book 'Ultimate Questions' in Bulgarian —like entrance tickets at the door! The demise of communism had left a vacuum in so many peoples lives, and many of those present were from the professional classes such as teachers, engineers, media people and even one sea captain. It seemed strange to me to be interviewed on Bulgarian radio during that week and asked about the relevance of the Christian faith for Bulgaria. How things had changed since they arrested us several years before, and deported us from the country.

I think the Lord must have a sense of humour, because the seating in this lower hall was very comfortable and had come from the former Communist Party Headquarters! The believers did not mind that the chairs had red leather cushions! I remember vividly one evening when the hall was full and the message was being preached. A man began calling out in an urgent way from the back of the hall. Pastor Godspodinov stood up and there was a two way conversation between him and the man at the back. Then the man fell on his knees and began to pray. As he did, from around the hall came the word 'Slava, slava' – Glory to God. The man had evidently called out for me to pray for him to be forgiven his sins, but the pastor was telling him to ask God for himself and seek his forgiveness and salvation. This he did, and I never did get to finish that sermon.

Alan Simmons, a very good friend from Bournemouth now began to join me on these preaching trips and as the Methodist church had opened in town, we were able to include this church into our programme.

The communists had confiscated the old Methodist church in the town, and turned it into a children's puppet theatre. Under the new law of restitution, the theatre had to be handed back to the handful of elderly Methodists that were still alive. The directors of the Puppet theatre were not keen about this, as you can imagine. The few Methodists that remained said that they did not want the children to be deprived of their theatre, but if a hall at the back of the theatre could be renovated for them, and light and heating be supplied then they would be happy. It was not an ideal building, with two small balconies one above the other that made the building look as high as it was long, but it served its purpose for a good number of years before the

Methodists were able to build a large new church in the centre of the city. It has a cross on the top that is even higher than the Orthodox Cathedral about half a mile away.

In order that the Methodist church could have a minister, the Baptist church released one of its deacons to pastor the church. It grew rapidly, and also planted some new churches in the villages.

There were some weeks of evangelism in those early days of freedom from communism, when there was hardly a night when we did not see people coming to the Lord. There were no big crowds, but there was a lovely sense of the presence of the Lord. I remember Allan coming back from preaching in the Methodist church one Sunday evening in utter astonishment, to say that there had been 14 people who had sought the Lord that night. What always impressed in those days was that when the pastor referred to such people he always spoke of them as those who 'had repented of their sins.'

One evening we were just about to leave the building when a man came hurrying back and was relieved to find that we were still there. He was a Russian dentist who had been in the meeting that night, and under deep conviction of sin had hurriedly left and started for home in his car. He stopped and returned to the church where we knelt on the floor with him as he cried to God to save him.

On the final night of this particular week of evangelistic meetings, after I had preached on the New Birth an old lady called out from the congregation, 'Am I too old to be born again? The pastor invited her forward for prayer, but for the next twenty minutes she recounted her life story of religious endeavour, from Orthodox church to Protestant and Baptist. But now she realised that she was not born again and wanted to experience God's forgiveness and salvation. As you can imagine there was great rejoicing as she sought the Lord in repentance.

Christian literature has been in short supply in this country and we had been able to help with the production of 10,000 copies of John Blanchard's excellent book 'Ultimate Questions, in the Bulgarian language. To a people who had never seen a Christian book, let alone a book that clearly spells out the gospel, this really was something to be savoured. I took a number of copies with me on the bus to town, and passed one to a man sitting beside me on the bus. He then waved this around and several other people then asked if they could have a copy. Going into a restaurant for lunch, when I paid the bill I gave the waitress a copy with her tip, and within minutes the chef came out and asked if he could have a copy, followed by the manager. All this is very different from the apathy in the U.K.

During these visits, I sometimes had a teacher of English from an Institute of Higher education translate for me. I asked her one day how she had become a Christian. She told me that back in 1989 a colleague had shared something of the gospel with her, but it was a dangerous thing to do in those days. However, when working as an interpreter on a Bulgarian ship she was given a Bible. Although it was very small print she started to read it beginning at Genesis. Being educated in the communist system she had been taught that Christianity was only a religious myth. Day after day she read this book very carefully. 'The Bible sounded like music to my ears,' she said. 'It was like finding another world.' Winter and summer passed and she continued reading, but now switched to the New Testament. 'The sermon on the mount turned me inside out as I read it over and over again until I could repeat it by heart. The simple question of Jesus in Matthew 6:27 asking If I could grow taller by worrying about it made me realise the absurdity of my whole life. Then I started to read the gospel of John, and as I read my heart began to change. It was when I read this gospel and what it said about Jesus that by the last verse I realised that Jesus was my personal Saviour, and I began to jump for joy. I had met God through His book, the Bible, and my life has been changed since that day. God's Word is indeed powerful and life changing.

John Ortburg in his book 'Living the Good life,' tells the story of a two week trek to Ethiopia during the communist days 'The underground churches had asked him to bring them some Bibles and although he had some reservation about smuggling Bibles he felt that God's people should not be deprived of the Word of God. Arriving at the border the customs official opened the suitcases and confiscated the Bibles. Several day later, he received a call saying that the head customs official wanted him to come for an interview.' He goes on to say that the official said 'these Bibles that I confiscated are illegal, but you can keep them on one condition – I want one for myself and you must say nothing about it.'

Return of the London Emmanuel Choir

Having taken about 30 members of the choir to Varna during the dark days of the communist regime, it was a great joy now that freedom had come to take a larger group of the choir to Varna, and to a wonderful opportunity to sing and preach the Gospel for two weeks.

Arriving at the airport on a Saturday afternoon we were greeted by the pastor and leaders of the First Baptist Church, and presented with bouquets of flowers. We then set off on our own two coaches to a large holiday resort about 15kms from Varna. Muriel Shepherd, the conductor of the choir, was with us and the choir had been able to learn some of their songs in the Bulgarian language. Mrs. Shepherd had insisted that the choir come complete with their choir uniforms which looked very spectacular.

During this period we were able to have several concerts at the First Baptist Church and also out in the villages with part of the choir. The Methodist church in town although small inside had tiered stone seating outside that could seat several hundred people. It was one of the first open air evangelistic meetings in the city. When the choir began to sing 'Amazing Grace' in Bulgarian it drew even more people from the nearby streets to come and listen. Each night when the choir had sung it was my joy to preach the gospel.

One afternoon we were able to go and sing in the local prison, and that came about because a very fine American young missionary had made good contact with the prison officers and was teaching a group of them English on a regular basis. I don't think that such a visit would be possible today, but then it was God's time for many of these hardened criminals to hear God's Word.

I noticed that afternoon when I was speaking, a prisoner sitting in the front row who looked as though he had recently damaged his arm. It was bandaged but bloodstained, and I enquired what had happened. He told me via my interpreter that he had been feeling very fearful because of his sins and so had cut his arm and shed his blood to find forgiveness. I asked him why did he think that he could be forgiven this way ? He replied that many years ago when he was a small boy, his grandmother had told him that 'Without the shedding of blood there is no forgiveness of sins.' I had just a few minutes to tell him that Jesus shed his blood on the cross and that was why he as a sinner could find forgiveness. He was quickly marched away by the guards and I have often wondered if he ever found forgiveness God's way.

When Allan Simmons had been with me two months before the Emmanuel Choir visit, we went one afternoon to visit the Manager of the Festival Hall near the sea side in Varna. It was a beautiful hall recently built with very comfortable tiered seating, a large stage that would house the choir and a beautiful pipe organ. We asked if it was possible to hire it for a choir concert and the answer was 'yes.' The price for the Saturday afternoon rehearsal and the Saturday evening concert was £50! We tried not to look surprised, booked and paid for the hall. Where would you get such a hall anywhere in our country for that price. The evening concert was tremendous and as well as many local people present we were able to bring down from the resort where we were staying some British Holiday makers.

The Hotel Staff where we were staying were intrigued to have such talented guests and one day asked if we would do a concert for the Hotel Staff and we could use the bandstand for the occasion. There were the waiters, chamber maids, office staff and porters, and then of course many folk on holiday hearing the choir singing came to listen. What we did not know was that on the level below the bandstand was the 'Red Lion' the only British Pub in Bulgaria, and the BBC were filming it for one of the holiday programmes. One of their camera crew came upstairs to us and was amazed to see a British Choir singing hymns – and in Bulgarian!

Bulgaria and Occultism

Before leaving home for what was to be my 33rd visit to Varna I had an urgent e-mail from the pastor of the 1st Baptist church to ask me to speak one evening on the dangers of the occult. Evidently, over the past six months there had been an onslaught of 'occult' activity in the country. Magazines and Newspapers were full of adverts inviting people to consult with a medium or fortune teller – for a price of course! Even the radio and Television feature weekly programmes on the subject. On street corners there are Tarot Card readers and read your future in the stars promotions. Spirit healers now abound because people are finding that the national health service is rather limited in what it can do for them – and the Devil also has power to heal. I noticed an advert outside a night club that said 'Come and dance with the Devil.'

In view of all of this the pastor of the church asked me to tackle the subject from a Biblical angle and he would then advertise the subject as 'The occult –is it fact or fiction.' A good crowd turned up at the church, many of them being people who were involved in the occult in some way, and the Lord greatly helped me in speaking on the subject.

I meet up with Georgi Todorov

On my arrival one year, and staying in the little seaside resort of St. Konstantine, I was delighted to find Georgi Todorov waiting for me at the Hotel desk. He is the son of the old pastor from the Varna Baptist church that was destroyed by the communists. I have known him since he was a small boy. During those difficult days he often told me that one day he would be a pastor, but in my wildest dreams I never imagined that it would ever be possible. With the fall of communism he was able to study at the London Bible College and now had taken up the responsibility of pastoring a church in the town of Sliven.

Driving across to Sliven he told me something of the make up of his little congregation. It had started about four years ago when a lady from Sliven had been converted after visiting a church in another city and hearing the gospel for the first time.(When I met her she told me that I had been the preacher on that occasion) Returning home to Sliven, she started Bible studies in her home and others were converted. Eventually an old house became available and with help from believers in other churches they had created a lovely little church building, none of the church members had been a Christian longer than four years!

Georgi still had his home city of Varna on his heart and after several years as pastor in Sliven he moved back to the city with his English wife Anne. With some other believers who had been involved with the old church in the city they began to pray about the possibility of starting a church back in the city. On the site of the old church that had been demolished by the communists, a block of flats had been built, so they looked for a small building that they might hire on Sunday mornings. Eventually they found a drinking club that they could hire for a reasonable price, and here they started a Sunday morning service. It was a fairly rough place and certainly smelt heavily of beer when Georgi and several others arrived early on a Sunday morning. All the windows were opened and the empty beer cans around were cleared away. It took quite a lot of elbow grease and hot water to make the room reasonably presentable for worship, but here they stayed for several years, though they could only meet on a Sunday morning.

The Gideons had been banned for a while after the fall of communism but now were legal and slowly had been trying to place New Testaments into some of the Varna Schools. A few days after the presentation of the Scriptures at one school some of the Testaments were found torn up and pressed down on spiked railings. On week later the class of boys and that had received the New Testaments went on a school trip by coach. Sadly, the coach crashed and 12 boys were killed and others seriously injured. It had, as you can imagine, a devastating effect on the school. We wondered if any of those kids had read anything of God's Word before they were ushered into eternity.

Church Plants

During my time with the lst Baptist church on the outskirts of the city I was asked to visit and preach in some of their church plants, mainly in gypsy villages. The small church in one village had been started by a man and his wife converted 8 years ago when I had an evangelistic mission in the city. The wife said to me, 'I repented of my sins on the 4th night of the mission.' They had started a micro-enterprise growing cabbages to sell in the market and the proceeds funded the work of the church.

In one gypsy village they asked me to speak on what the Bible says about marriage. The reason being that in this village none of them get married! It is too expensive because you have to invite the whole village to the feast! Even the gypsy mayor came for the evening to hear what I had to say on the subject. At the end of the service I was asked to pray for the one married Christian young lady who still had no child even after five years of marriage. You can imagine what a challenge this was to her faith because all the single girls had children —many of them after seeking help from a medium!

An interesting church plant was in a flat on the 5th floor of a block of flats. Guests could come up in the lift or the stairs without being seen by the neighbours. Two rooms in the flat had been knocked together so that between 30-40 people could be seated.

The Methodist church also had a number of exciting church plants and in one gypsy village they had built their own brick church. It was a joy to be invited over a number of years to spend some time with them preaching the gospel. We started the meetings when everybody had come in from the fields and tethered their donkeys. The pastor much to the amusement of my interpreter introduced me as Billy Graham. He had evidently had only ever heard of one evangelist and as I was an evangelist then I must be Billy Graham. In the end I gave up correcting him—even though he introduces me in the same way every time I preach in his church!

I was back in the church one year when towards the end of my message the pastor was called out and then in the final hymn came back and announced that the Tent had come! Evidently once a year a German Christian Organisation brought a Circus Tent to Bulgaria and planted it in different villages. It came with men who erected it and there were 200 seats plus amplification equipment, and even a video projector and several gospel films with Bulgarian captions. So at the end of the service we all trooped down to the centre of the village where this beautiful multi-coloured tent was erected.

My translator at this point was being spoken to and then she turned to me and said, 'the pastor says that God has answered his prayers and would I preach in the Tent for the next three nights?' My response was a resounding 'Yes,' I would love to preach in the Tent.' So for the next three nights in a Circus Tent, packed with best part of the population of the village I preached the gospel. In fact I had to speak twice each night. First of all to the children of the village and then to the adults, although some of the children crept back in and sat on the ground. The pastor's wife fed me on bacon and eggs each night before preaching. She evidently fried it back at the church, and then carried it down to the Tent, by which time it was rather cold —but I ate it!

By book 'Go for growth' was now published in Bulgaria by the newly established Christian Publishing House and churches were using it in many parts of the country. I was highly amused one evening when an old lady from the Methodist church spoke to me with some bewilderment. How was it that after many years of visiting her country I still could not speak the language, but could write the language so well! It took several minutes to explain to her that the book had been very well translated for me by a lovely Christian lady who had not long been a Christian herself.

Georgi Todorov's faith rewarded

The communists had destroyed the Varna Baptist church buiding. Now after meeting on a Sunday morning in a drinking club, the fellowship led by George had a plot of land that stood vacant right beside where the old church had been. But on each side of the plot, flats had been built by the city council. Planning and building permission would only be granted on the understanding that the new church would have to be as high as the flats. All of this would of course add to the cost involved in building. An old property became available at the rear and the church was able to buy it and then demolish it, giving them a little more room.

There was no way in which they could meet on the site at this point and so they built a single story hall on this land and it seats about 100, and here they have been meeting as the new church is being built. What was remarkable was that they managed to get this small hall built in 40 days, and it really is a lovely building.

Because of its height(4 storey) the new Baptist church will be able to cater for a soup kitchen, plus medical rooms for dentistry and a doctor, main auditorium and youth hall, plus offices. It is planned to serve the community as well as being a place where the Word of God is preached.

It now has all of its windows in place -72 in all, and all double glazed. As you can imagine, there is so much more to do inside the building.Usually in Bulgaria, when they build a new church they move into the lower hall when it is finished and then as they are able to gradually work their way up to the top of the building.

In the meantime the church has grown and have been given a set of hand bells by an American Group and now have a fine handbell choir. They not only play in the church but also have been playing after dinner at several tourist hotels. I would never have thought during the communist regime that I would every sit in a Bulgarian Hotel and hear the hymn 'What a friend we have in Jesus' played on hand bells.

Although the Christians are working slowly and patiently on their new building they are seeking ways of reaching out into their community with the gospel. Georgi has translated 'Christianity Explored' into Bulgarian and it seems as though when one course is finished another one starts. Those that attend are young adults, most of whom would never come into church on a Sunday. So George now has two congregations, and trying to bring them together is very difficult. One couple who attend own a Hotel in the city but never miss an evening study during the week. One evening when I joined them for the study, George told me that he was going to speak briefly (it turned out to be for 40 minutes) and then I was to speak followed by questions.

Helping an orphanage in Rudnick

The church has also been reaching out to help an orphanage about 40 kms from Varna. With some help also from some British churches during the past few years, play rooms for the children and also toilets and shower rooms have been built. All this care has made a profound impression upon the local officials. I happened to be visiting on the day that the toilets were going to be dedicated ! The local Mayor, Director of Social Services for Varna and several other officials were in attendance.. I have been present at a number of dedications of buildings, but never to dedicate toilets! After the dedication, the director of social services hosted a champagne reception in the office of the director of the orphanage.

I have been much impressed by the dedication and love of the staff for the children, many of whom have either physical or mental problems. The love, concern and practical help that has been given to the staff thorough the church has given George and those of us who visit a wonderful platform to share the gospel with them.

As a result of the churches involvement in helping the orphanage, the local mayor of the village of Rudnick said that the old theatre could be used for four nights for meetings, and if some printing was done to advertise the meetings then she would herself personally take it round the village and invite people to attend. – and they did come. On the opening night I counted 180 people – and as far as I know all of them would have been unconverted people. I could never remember an evangelistic meeting where the audience were all in need of this life transforming gospel.

By the second and third night we were able to bring across some Bulgarian Bibles and copies of different Gospels also in Bulgarian. The orphanage staff took turns to come to the meetings. Some of these village people now come down by mini-bus to the church in Varna. I think that I had an important principle underlined to me at Rudnick, and it was that you must win the right to preach the gospel, and this was certainly the case in Rudnick.

Now there is a Bible study that runs in the village and those that attend are some who found the Lord in those remarkable few days of evangelism in the old theatre.

Imaginative evangelism is also pursued by George. One morning he invited me to go with him and his father to 'Bless a Boutique' in a 5 star Hotel in Golden Sands. The Orthodox priests visit businesses, and even homes to bless them – at a price! Bulgarians are nominally Orthodox, but also very superstitious, so they happily pay up. George offers this service free and so I went with him on this occasions. The boutique was right in the middle of a large Hotel foyer and it really looked attractively set out. I recognised the owner as a lady from the church. She had been converted several years ago so it was a joy to see her again. George read from the Bible and then his dad prayed for the lady and the staff. Refreshments were served and then the staff were given Bulgarian Bibles – and on we were to the next similar event in another Hotel.

I met him by a swimming pool

Staying in a small Holiday complex about 8kms from Varna and sitting b y a swimming pool, a young Bulgarian man asked me if I would speak to him in English to try and improve his knowledge of our language. When he moved on, an older man sitting nearby asked if he could try and improve his English. After quickly discovering that he was a Christian. He told me that with the help of his sons he was trying to put a brief Bulgarian translation onto an English copy of the Jesus film. He then told me that he was the secretary of the Bible Society of Christian Unity. However in secular life he was the Vice Dean of the Medical Institute of the Bulgarian Academy of Sciences. He had only become a Christian four years previously on a visit to Munich in West Germany to give a medical lecture, and then found his way into a Christian Bookshop. The owners befriended him and led him Christ.

Just about this time I had become involved with the Christian Television Association in producing missionary documentaries in different parts of the world for UFM Worldwide. Subsequently, for a number of years I was the Chairman of the CTA. I then suggested to the doctor that it might be possible to bring a camera crew to Bulgaria and produce a film in the Bulgarian language. I then asked him that if it happened would he be prepared to present it on camera. His response was immediate – 'Yes, I would.'

At this point all I could say was that I would pursue the possibility when I was back in England the following week. Returning home, I quickly rang the cameraman director of CTA and his response was that they would make such a film at half price £4000. Sunday evening I was in my home church in Leicester and while reporting on the visit mentioned the possibility of making a film for the Bulgarian church to use in their evangelism. Monday evening a friend rang to say that the money was available.

It was then important to travel to Sofia to see what and how we should film. Detcho Slivinov our film presenter was not willing to miss out on my presence and invited me to give a series of lectures on Christian foundational truths at the University. However, it was now winter time and when I arrived late one evening the temperature had dropped drastically. Not to be beaten by the weather, Detcho quickly managed to lay on some evangelistic meetings at both the Pentecostal and Baptist Churches. Attendances were excellent, with every seat taken and many standing for the whole service. It was the first time that I had preached with a warm overcoat on, plus a thick jumper and a scarf.

When the better weather came a few months later, cameraman director, sound man and myself were able to travel to Sofia and in one week managed to make a film that we entitled 'The Relevance of Christianity in Bulgaria Today.' Detcho did a superb job in presenting it and he also took us to Bulgarian Television where we met several high officials of their Television NetWork. When we told them that we would like them to have our film they told us that they could not afford it 'No price to you.' We told them, and they were more than happy to accept a Betamax copy that was subsequently screened on National Television. Later on it was possible to get 500 video copies for the churches to use in their evangelism.

An amazing opportunity

On the last Saturday night of our filming, Detcho rang me at the Hotel where we were staying to ask me if I would preach at a very special rally on the Sunday morning. It would be in the former Communist Party Hall in the centre of the city. The communist party had just that week handed it over to the mayor of Sofia. Detcho knew the mayor and suggested I could be invited to speak as a special guest from England! As you can imagine I did not need asking twice.

This was the hall where the communist deputies once sat. The seating was on leather backed chairs, maybe a thousand of them. The lighting came from massive crystal chandeliers. The stage was where the Politburo sat and Zhikov, the party secretary made his speeches glorifying communism and denying God or the relevance of the gospel. On top of the stage, high up near the roof was the hammer and sickle and a bust of Lenin.

On the stage was a large choir who sang beautifully. There was not a lot of congregational singing as so many of the audience were non-Christians, but there was a lovely sense of the presence of God. That Sunday morning, in such a place, I was able to preach on 'God's forgiveness, the greatest gift in the world.'

The leader of the meeting made an appeal to people to repent of their sins and they were called to come and kneel in front of the platform and ask God to forgive them. I noticed one very well dressed man with his arms round a gypsy man and praying for him. I wondered who he was and was told that he was the Brazilian Ambassador, a very fine Christian from the Pentecostal church. God has His people in all professions and all over the world.

But where did George Todorov come into the story? We who were making the film did not understand the Bulgarian language so how could we possibly edit the film accurately and put in the necessary linking up of the material? Just at that time George was in England studying at the London Bible College, so we were able to bring him into the studio to help with the editing and to record the necessary link ups. God has His ways, His timing and His people just when they are needed.

It has been a privilege to have visited this country 36 times and to have seen yet again that God's Word does not need defending, it just needs to be preached. The Bible with its life transforming message travels well in the land of Bulgaria.

9

Constanta in Romania

During the early days of my visits to Christians in Bulgaria, I began to ask questions about the country of Romania that was north of Bulgaria. I was told about the Baptist church in Constanta, a large port also on the Black Sea Coast. Bulgarian believers told me about the church and gave me the names and addresses of several key people in the church, but they added please be careful if you visit their homes. So after two weeks in Varna I returned home to the UK and then a month later returned to Gatwick, and this time a flight on Romanian Airways.

This was my first visit to Romania. Package holidays were always the safest way to visit the communist countries. Their planes were usually crammed to capacity and arrived in Romania in the middle of the night. However, to-night was going to be like no other flight. My flight number being called I walked down as instructed to gate 14 to find that I was the only person there. Ten minutes later, an elderly couple came along and then a man with a pronounced limp, followed by a single lady of uncertain years. The flight was called again, but no further passengers arrived! I thought that I must have come to the wrong gate, but an official told me that this was the gate. Glistening on the tarmac was a Boeing 707, and we were the total passenger compliment for the flight. In fact,there were more crew on the plane than passengers!

As I settled back in my seat in the near empty jet, I could not help smiling at the thought of being transported 'executive style' across Eastern Europe. This at great expense to the communist system to help and encourage those that the system was trying to destroy. I think sometimes that our God has a lovely sense of humour. I even managed to doze off to sleep – a thing I rarely do when flying. I was awakened by the stewardess requesting us to fasten our seat belts for landing at Constanta airport.

It was now nearly 3am and was rather chilly when I stepped out of the aircraft and down the steps. As always, one was greeted or maybe more accurately to say –confronted by a galaxy of officialdom. Soldiers, police and other officials with no known title. The five of us were escorted to a waiting airport bus as if we were a plane load of passengers and driven the few hundred yards to the airport terminal. Security checks for weapons was no problem as our cases were being put through X-Ray machines and these did not show up God's Word, in fact the official did not even look at the screen when the cases were put through.

Passport control was slow but straight forward, and then to my joy a porter picked up my luggage and carried it to the customs official who looked in sheer disbelief at 5 passengers on a Boeing 707 – scratched his head and waved us through. What I had thought would have been a problem with so few of us on the flight turned out to be a blessing in disguise. Our God is good in every way, and it was good to be reminded yet again that 'Our times are in His hands.'

First contact

I had been given the name and address of the family Topov, but the whereabouts of their street in the city I had no clue. So, my first morning I went down into Constanta to try and buy a street map. When I did manage to buy one, it was very limited and basically only highlighted the tourist spots. The second day I caught the trolley bus to town and walked most of the day looking for the street on which the family lived. I had been told that the street was off the main road into town, but all to no avail.

By now it was Sunday morning and I did so much want to find the church. Sitting in my Hotel room I just cried to God for help. It seemed to be so sad to have managed to bring in the much needed Word of God in the Romanian language and now have no one to pass it on to. I can remember saying, 'Lord, I'll try just once more, and if I have drawn a blank then I guess it was not your will to come here and I've made one big mistake.

Jumping on the first bus that came along I headed off down to the city, praying all the way. Suddenly I felt an impulse to get off the bus and only just made it before the automatic doors closed. Looking up at the street name, to my amazement it was the very street that I had been looking for during the past two days. Fifty yards up the street was the house number that I needed. I remember an old Christian saying to me, 'God sometime waits until the last train, but He always catches it.' Taking the piece of paper with the name written on it, I gingerly knocked on the door. A small sleepy eyed boy opened the door and then swiftly closed it. Not a good start- so I tried again, because before the lad had closed the door I had seen what I was sure was a text on the hall wall, so I knocked again.

This time a stocky man in trousers and vest opened the door. I showed him the name on the paper and he immediately smiled and pulled me inside and shut the door. Out of another room came a stout, smiling lady who turned out to be his wife – but alas neither could speak a word of English.

Nothing daunted the good lady sat me down with a cup of coffee and speedily left the room to telephone someone. Coming back into the room she indicated that I was to go with her, so swallowing my scalding hot coffee I joined her as she walked up to the bus stop and on to a bus, this time going through Constanta and out into the country. Getting off the bus it was a walk across a field, down a dirty lane and into the courtyard of a small church. I was taken round the back to be greeted by a young married woman, who, when my guide spoke to her turned and spoke to me in what sounded like French. They thought that I had come from France! So it appeared to be a wasted journey, but not really, because with the aid of a writing pad and pencil I managed to draw a rough map of the British Isles and then the word-England. It was not long before someone was produced who spoke English, and by then it was time to leave for the evening service at the Baptist Church in town.

Brother Topov that I had met early in the morning when I called at his house turned out to be a deacon at the church as well as the orchestra conductor and youth leader(unofficial of course). The children of his family all played musical instruments. Although I visited this family many times over the next few years, we always recounted with great amusement our first meeting with all of its frustration. One of the daughters now speaks English reasonable well, so visiting the home is not such a strain. Of course I was relieved to be able to leave my precious cargo, small as it was with the family and they knew how to move it out quickly.

On one occasion when I was in Constanta, I went to the church first of all instead of to my friend's house, and once again saw the wisdom of God in His perfect timing. Folk at the church warned me not to visit the home because the father was in trouble with the authorities and there was a strong suspicion that the house was being closely watched by the police and might even be bugged. It turned out that the family were living in the same house that a well known Romanian Christian leader had lived in a few years before.

Evidently one morning the secret police had arrived on the doorstep and thoroughly searched the house, taking papers, books, tapes, Bibles and music books. All the members of the family were interrogated separately and very cleverly. One of the younger children cracked when threats were made about what they would do to his father. When folk from the church told me what had happened I felt so thankful to God for the privilege of living in a free country where practising your faith is not a crime – as yet!

For some months after that traumatic day, one of the family Topov was in a very nervous state and had to have medical help. It also meant the end of her hopes for a place at University. Father Topov lost his job and was transferred to a lower paid job.

Renewing fellowship

Back in Constanta the next year my plane from Gatwick never landed until 3am, but on arriving at my hotel the bleary eyed girl at the reception desk had no note of my arrival or booking, and so there was no room available for me. On producing a receipt that carried the name of the hotel plus the date, I was eventually found a room and fell exhausted into bed.

At mid- afternoon on Sunday, I made my way down to the church for the evening service. The first time back after a year is always strange during the communist days. Would the building still be open? I arrived about 5pm. Although the services do not begin until 6pm the church was already beginning to fill up. One old lady escorts me to a seat. In this church the men sit on one side and the ladies on the other.

By 5-30pm, it looks though every seat is occupied, but as the seats are pews, you have to keep trying to move a little nearer to the next person. The older ladies dress sombrely and wear headscarves tied tightly round their heads. Before taking their seats they stand and pray quietly. Up above, the planks of the balcony groaned under the weight of a hundred or so people. At the front, and surrounding the pulpit was the young people's orchestra – about 30 of them playing mandolins and balalikas, and the sound was wonderful as they accompany the choir.

The pastor of the church together with a retired pastor, now come up into the pulpit and this was the signal for every one to stand up. The pastor leads fervently in prayer and there was a loud amen from all the congregation. A hymn was announced and they really do know how to sing in harmony in this church. It may have been a little slow compared to the way we sing our hymns, but I think I prefer it this way, it is far more worshipful. By the way, the people sit to sing and stand for prayer and the reading of the Bible.

Tonight I am told is a special evangelistic service so there was a programme of items. First of all the choir sang and this was followed by a Bible recitation. The orchestra then played their own arrangement of 'Master the Tempest is raging.' We then stood for prayer and the pastor preached. I couldn't understand a word as far as the language was concerned, but I felt its power in my heart and saw its effect upon the congregation.

When the pastor finished shaking hands with all the people that he could reach at the entrance, he came to speak to me in his clipped English. His first question was 'can you stay for the week and preach at some meetings.' In a few minutes my diary was full for the week. My last Sunday would be a day that I would not easily forget. It was to be the baptism of some people, young and old who had recently been converted. When I asked how many, the pastor said that there were only 65 this time! As you can imagine the service was very lengthy as each one gave a brief testimony. The singing was electrifying and then the pastor preached, so it was about 10pm before it all finished. I slipped out quietly and walked down the very dark street to the main road. There at the bus stop I had a renewed confidence in the power of this glorious gospel that was making such an impact in the lives of so many Romanian people.

David and Christina a young couple that I had met on a previous visit to Constanta had asked me to visit their home on a Monday evening and the sun was shining brightly when I set off for town. As they told me that their street was only about 2kms down the main road and a turning on the left I decided to walk. It was a broad road with two lane traffic each way, but hardly any traffic, and the first car I saw was stopped by the police! The reason became obvious about a half a kilometre ahead – a police radar trap! They are the same the world over!

Buses coming out from the city were already beginning to look full. Work for some factory workers was finished for the day, but for others it was only the second part of the working day as the shops began to open.

Some of the men were already outside the beer shops having their daily Guiness or whatever it was called in this part of the world – and some of them looked as if they had already drunk a week's ration. Old ladies with gnarled faces and thick black stockings were passing the time of day outside their houses and smartly dressed young people were leaving the buses and hastening down the side streets to their homes.

Outside one small house was a great pile of logs and two men had a wonderful contraption fixed on the pavement sawing them up into more manageable proportions. The old petrol engine that operated the monster, coughed and spluttered from time to time as some logs proved to be too large and tough to cut. Meanwhile an old donkey that was obviously used to pulling the contraption around stood quite unconcerned by all the noise, smoke and petrol fumes –but then possibly by now he was stone deaf!

Coming to the street in which my friends lived, I turned off the broad boulevard and down a dark narrow lane with many trees on both sides. I was glad of their shade, not so much from the sun as from the glances of people who would have recognised me as not belonging in their street. The house I wanted was some distance down, but it was not difficult to find as like many East European houses there was not only the number of the house but the family name as well.

Their home was a little bungalow, two bedrooms, a living room cum-dining room, a bathroom, toilet and a small kitchen. Everything was spotlessly clean inside. On the largest wall of the living room was a large pictorial Turkish carpet depicting the Last Supper. In one corner was a rather battered upright piano on which perched a Sony tape recorder that I had been able to bring on my last visit. In the centre of the room was a round table and when I arrived David was typing and making 8 carbon copies of a Christian book recently translated into Romanian. Immediately I was reminded of the famine of Christian literature that there is in this country. My mind raced back to the shelves of books in my study library at home and to the thousands of Christian books of every conceivable type in Christian Bookshops.

David and Christina are a lovely young couple and they both come from Christian families. Christina is of Russian origin and so speaks the language fluently. They have a lovely three year old daughter and a second child was expected shortly. David has a good job as an engineer, but most of his spare time is taken up with the Lord's work. His boss had been brought up in a salvation army home and so had a sneaking admiration for believers, so David had few problems at work.

We sat and talked about the situation of believers and their current problems. Increasing negative comments in the press and radio had been directed against believers. Several strange religious sects were being highlighted and the suggestion made that Baptists were part of a sect. One such sect that was being publicised was called 'Underground Church of God.' They didn't marry but just co-habited. They literally dug caves and lived underground together as a commune. Their children were made to fast and one such child had recently died of malnutrition. The authorities were linking the sect with a similar group in the USA. So you can see how subtle the Devil is in using the title 'The Underground Church.'

David told me about a recent visit with his older brother to some of the villages where there are no churches, but many believers. Meanwhile Christina had been busy in her small kitchen and now brought in her culinary creation and set the table for supper. After standing for a long grace we sat down and shared a lovely meal of freshly cooked fish from the lake, with cheese, bread and ham, followed by cake and grapes.

Supper being ended the lid of the old piano was opened and Christina began to play some hymns. The small daughter came out of her shell and so came and stood by the piano and sang 'Maranatha, Hallelujah.' I thought back to most British Church Sunday Schools where crowds of children would be singing choruses. This little lass never at this time had an opportunity to join in such activity, but her parents had taught her to sing about the second coming of the Lord Jesus Christ.

The singing brought in Christina's old mother from across the alleyway. Father was in bed, nearly totally paralysed after a stroke and they told me that he was dying. He indicated that the door to his room be open so that he could hear the singing,. David then said that his wife and mother would sing an old Russian hymn about God being with us in the storms of life and it was just beautiful harmony.

Father wanted to see me, so we went across the dark narrow alley and into a little bedroom. The old man remembered my face from a previous visit to the church, but not my name. I shared a promise from God's Word. He whispered a word or two in Romanian and David translated it to me. We prayed together and all of this by interpretation while the little grand daughter played happily on her dying grandfather's bed – totally oblivious that he was just about to pass into his Saviour's presence.

Mother stood there still and quiet, while Christina sobbed uncontrollably. It was a solemn and yet triumphant moment. I said no more but quickly stepped out of the room down the alley, back up the narrow lane to the boulevard and then back on the bus to the hotel. Yes, the Bible travels well at the bedside of an old Romanian believers just about to pass across into Heaven.

Divine originality

It was a hot sultry morning. The beach was as usual crowded with tourists from all over Europe and also of course some Romanian citizens on holiday. Brother A. had arranged to meet some of the brethren down on the sands for a time of fellowship and conversation and about eight of them sat around talking happily. The suggestion was made that they pray before leaving and this was readily agreed to so one after another led in prayer. When it came to brother A. he prayed in a loud voice and it quickly became apparent that he was not praying but preaching to the other men on the beach!

The situation could be dangerous now. One of the group gave a signal and the preaching stopped, but not for long because brother A strode down the beach into the sea. Many people followed him as he proceeded to carry on the message waist deep in the sea for another five minutes! Little did I ever think that I would see the message of the gospel and the Bible travel waist deep into the Black Sea! Some of the brothers told me that he was always doing something unusual in order to bring something of the gospel to the people of his land. I guess that you might say that it was a bit of Divine originality!

A flight with a difference

It was the normal 'Tarom' Romanian airways flight from Gatwick to Constanta. For this trip I had packed away a good quantity of New Testaments for new Christians so at least they could have some part of the Word of God. I knew from previous trips that customs security was very little, so I also put some in my hand luggage. About 15 minutes from landing a lady sitting on her own near the front, suddenly jumped up with what looked like a gun. In an instant two men sitting in the front row grabbed her and flung her to the ground. As they spoke Romanian it was evident that they were security men as they spoke with the crew in their language.

When we landed, as you can imagine the plane was surrounded by soldiers and police and we were all escorted off to the control zone and joined a queue to have our luggage searched (even though we did learn later that the poor lady had only a replica gun and was evidently mentally disturbed.)

All suitcases were being carefully searched and even some cases emptied. My mouth went dry and I am sure that my heart was beating faster as I got nearer to the table where the search was being conducted. In front of me was a lady whose luggage was being taken apart and then she was having great difficulty in getting it all back in her suitcase. I found myself, before she had finished, pushing my case forward to the officer, but to my amazement in his frustration with getting the poor lady to repack her suitcase, signalled to me to go straight through untouched. You can imagine that I didn't wait around but hurried through, and all my precious cargo of God's Word was safe and sound.

My final visit

Before I went to Romania for the first time I met in England a Romanian pastor named Josef Ton. He had come to Oxford to study theology and in the days that lay ahead he was to become one of the leaders of the Romanian Baptist Church during the later days of communism. Returning to Romania after his studies , he spent most of his time preaching the gospel and also standing up to the authorities. He became so well known in the West that the communists seemed to be afraid to touch him.

Now I was back in Constanta again. And on Sunday morning returned on the bus down to the church in plenty of time. I had job to get a seat until someone found one for me right in the front row of the church. Imagine my surprise when into the pulpit climbed Josef Ton. He had evidently been preaching every night for two weeks and this was the beginning of the third week. He suddenly saw me and invited me up into the pulpit to bring a greeting which I was glad to do. He then asked me if I would be there for the evening service and when I said yes he replied 'then you will preach tonight!

After the Sunday evening service Josef asked if I could stay with him for the week. Could I preach for him as he was feeling very tired, so it was my privilege to preach the gospel for the next six nights with Josef translating for me. It was an amazing scene each night. Not only was every seat occupied in the church and balcony but also younger people stood all around the sides of the buildings and even up the pulpit step and even spilled out into the foyer.

I noticed that two men were sitting at the front with a reel to reel tape recorder so imagined that they were recording the message for the benefit of older people who could not attend. However Josef told me that they were not from the church but from the secret police. Josef added, 'you will be safe because they know that you are with me.' I must confess that I did not feel very safe when he told me that!

Night after night we not only sensed the presence of the Holy Spirit in the meetings, but the response to the gospel amazed me. The invitation was given by Josef for people to repent of their sins and cry to the Lord to save and forgive them – and they did from all over the church.

One night when the choir was singing, Josef took me downstairs to a lower hall which was packed out with people on their knees crying out to God to save people who were listening to the Word preached upstairs. Josef, when he saw my astonished look said, 'this is why we are seeing so much blessing upstairs in the church.'

Another day I was invited to have a meal before the evening meeting at the house where Josef and his wife Elizabeth were staying. When I arrived, Elizabeth was there, but no Josef. When I asked after him she said, 'He's been at the Police Station all day' I then hastily suggested that maybe I should not come down to the church that night let alone preach when I only had a tourist visa and no permission to preach. But as we were talking Josef came in with a smile on his face and said that the policemen were doing the recording each night were complaining because Romania were playing an important football match that evening and they wanted to watch it on the T.V. They also wanted to know who was going to pay for the recording tape, to which Josef had told them that the church would pay. To my great relief they had asked him nothing about me.

As this was going to be my last night he asked me if I would take to England a translation of the book 'The Cross and the Switchblade' into

Romanian and send it to a publisher in America. How could I refuse? Then he asked me what time my flight was after the final meeting. To my horror, when he said goodbye publicly on behalf of the church he told them what time my flight was leaving! I imagined that the security officers would be waiting for me at the airport and that would be a disaster, but there was no such hold up. I got on the plane and arrived safely home – but this was to be my last visit to Romania.

10

India - You Love It or Hate It

I was told this before my first visit to India in 1985, and I must confess that I fell in love with that country or rather with the people.One billion live in this fascinating country and your first impression when you arrive, is that you are meeting them all at the same time.

From the noisy, bustling, and sometimes sweltering hot cities to the slower pace of thousands of villages, Indians are warm friendly people with a smile and a welcome wherever you go.This was true over many visits with my 'Christian Ministries' colleague Derek Cleave.

The invitation to go for the first time came from the 'India Fellowship of Bible Churches.' Founded in 1983, it is an Indian planted church fellowship with hundreds of village churches associated with it. The leader was a remarkable old Indian Pastor named Devasahayam meaning 'God is my helper.' After studying at Bible College he was seven years into his ministry before he was 'born again.' After serving for many years as the secretary of the Hyderabad Bible Society he started this fellowship of Bible believing churches.

Going for the first time to such a country, we did not know what to expect or where we would go during out stay. We did know that we would be met at Madras Airport- and so we were. Walking across the tarmac we could see a mass of people waiting to greet relatives and friends – it was just a sea of faces.

As we reached the barrier some smiling men greeted us warmly with necklaces of flowers, and I heard a disembarking westerner saying to his wife, 'They must be ambassadors!'- and of course we were. After a restful night (our last in a hotel) we set of on a train going north, and heading eventually to a village called Pangaluru. For the next week we were to hold Bible teaching sessions for just over one hundred pastors from village churches. They had come by bus or bicycle, and some had walked over 50 miles to be present.

During the day, from breakfast until late afternoon we taught the Word of God. Sitting on the floor with their large Telegu Bibles in front of them, it was a great joy to share God's Word with these pastors. There were also a few Bible women who worked amongst the women in the villages.

But what should we eat?

While the studies were taking place on the roof of the building under a tarpaulin cover, down in the courtyard food was being prepared on a large open huge cooking pot. The chef was a local Moslem man. He was most friendly and would not miss cooking for the annual conference. With his two lady assistants he turned out mountains of rice and curry twice a day.

We had been warned that it was not wise to eat this village curry as it would be too hot and spicy for us and so we heeded the warning. Rice would be safe enough, so would some carrots that we saw being cut up. Seeing some hard boiled eggs we indicated that we could eat them. It was an interesting meal even if rather bland, but we thanked our kind hosts and wondered what would be on offer at the next meal. It was exactly the same as the first meal. Rice, carrots and hard boiled eggs(two at a time) Eating so many eggs each day meant that most nights as we prepared for bed we sang 'bind us together! It was a salutary reminder that in the third world food is very basic and very repetitive because there is nothing else to eat. We did decide that on future visits we would take a supply of cup-a-soups to provide variety of taste.

On our next trip we were to stay in Secundrabad for a few days of meetings. Brother Dev, as we now called the leader of the village churches, put us into a hotel on the outskirts of the city. We had travelled from London to Bombay, and then flown down to Secundrabad. Owing to a six hour delay on Air India we arrived at our first meeting in time to give the benediction!

Returning to our hotel later than evening and feeling a little hungry, I went down to the desk to ask if the restaurant was open. I was greeted by the receptionist with the reply that the restaurant was closed because it was winter. But if I rang room service from our room then it would be possible to get some food.

Quite some time after ringing for room service a small Indian boy arrived, immaculately dressed in a red jacket and told me that he was John Paul the Second, to which I replied, ' and I am Ian Paisley,' which of course meant nothing to him. He then said that he would bring the menu for room service. After a wait of about twenty minutes he appeared carrying a massive menu —all of it in Chinese — with English sub-titles. I did a double take to see if we really were in India, but looking out of the window and seeing bullock carts coming slowly by, came to the conclusion that we were really were in India.

Finally deciding on some chicken noodle soup as being safe, our food fixer went on his way. After nearly an hour and just about giving up hope for any food, there was a knock on the door and in came our little waiter with two bowls. What was in them I am not sure, but it certainly was not the soup that we had ordered, it looked more like rice pudding, but we were hungry so we ate it-and went to bed.

We were up early and plunged into the programme with an 8-30am Bible study for Pastors and Christian leaders in the large Wesleyan Methodist Church. This was followed by an evangelistic rally each evening. One evening the Christian Headmistress from the girls High school brought the whole school and it was an impressive sight to see the girls taking up one whole side of the church.

In the city is a Theological College and we were invited to address the student body. As an optional extra on Saturday morning, I was invited to speak on 'sex in the church.' It was rather a challenge with only an hour to prepare. I had not been told before, what my subject would be. With a Bible and with God's instructions for every aspect of human life and relationships you could not go far wrong in turning them to God's Word.

Care for lepers

In this city of Hyderabad there was also a leper colony that brother Dev and his colleagues were interested in, and we had an exciting Saturday morning speaking at a hastily arranged meeting in their little church. None of the adults had any employment because they were lepers, so their occupation was begging on the streets of the city. Down in the city, in a very poor area, the Indian Fellowship of Bible Churches had managed to rent a small building. On the ground floor they had started a school, so that the children of lepers could have a basic education plus one meal a day consisting of a banana and a bread roll. Uniforms were bought for them and the parents made sure that they attended, and that there were no discipline problems. After all, if the children did well they could eventually be a 'meal ticket' for their parents.

Above the school room and up some very unsafe stairs, was the little church for lepers. On a Sunday morning the adults with the inevitable children would come upstairs for a service. Some of the adults were horribly disfigured but their children were healthy. The disease of leprosy is now well tackled in India, but the fruits of the disease from the days when there was little medical help could be seen in the adults. What we did notice in this service was the challenge of seeing these lepers, some with very disfigured and twisted hands putting their Sunday offering on the plate. Brother Dev told us that they gave from what they had begged on the streets during the past week. He later told us that percentage wise their giving was as good if not better than some similar congregations with members who did have a job and earned a salary.

Back on the train

From Secundrabad we had a nine hour train journey across the vast rolling plains of India, and that really was an experience. Village after village, fields, rivers, stations and the inevitable crowds of people. Every station sees an army of traders get on board and you could buy a cup of tea poured from a huge kettle. The seller only had three cups, so when one person had drunk their tea, the cup was passed to the next one unwashed! On the platform, a man was frying eggs on a metal plate over a gas burner and then if you bought one, it would be handed to you on a paper plate through the train window.

On the platform information monitor, to my astonishment, Chelsea was displayed playing Spurs! As the train slowly moved away with the tea seller still on board he was frantically trying to rescue his three cups and managed to step off the train just before it reached the end of the platform! Yes, India is a very different place. One little lad sat down beside me at one stage of the journey and talked to me about cricket and how India had recently beaten England. He even knew the names of our team, which was more than I did.

When we eventually arrived at an East coast town we were met and bundled into a dilapidated van that was to be our means of transport for the next eight days. It officially seated ten, but most nights going out to the villages for evangelistic meetings we managed to jam 19 into it. One night the lights failed, and the driver found his way down the track and across the fields with the aid of a torch.

The programme for the eight days was basically the same each day. Bible teaching for the pastors in the morning, then lunch followed by more Bible studies until about 4pm. After a short rest it was back into the van and off to a different village each evening. When we arrived we were safely placed in a hut away from the wondering gaze of the villagers – most of them had evidently never seen a white person before. After a meal of rice and vegetables prepared by our chef who had travelled with us, the meeting would get under way. In the centre of the village a large canvas sacking was stretched out on bamboo poles and this served as the roof for the meeting place. A battery operated loudspeaker boomed out an invitation to the village – and we were told that the majority of the villagers would attend. There was nothing else to do in the village after work in the surrounding fields was finished for the day. After some preliminary singing we both preached to a very attentive audience and it was a joy to know of a number each night, who we were told had repented of their sins and cried out to God for salvation.

In one village a lovely Indian widow who was a Christian, sold her wedding jewellery so as to hire a tent for the preaching of the gospel. She also paid for the hire of a tractor and cart to take us through the village in order to call the villagers to come and hear what we had to say. She also provided food for the group of pastors who came with us to the meetings to help with the singing and the music.

In one village I was preaching late at night, when at the end of the message a small baby was placed in my arms and my translator told me that I was to name the baby. With no time to think I prayed and named the baby Peter! Later on my colleague Derek Cleave said to me, 'But you didn't ask if it was a boy or a girl, then suggested that in 15 years time some lovely Indian girl would be living in the village with the name of Peter!

I must confess that Derek and I wondered how people hearing the gospel for the first time could be converted. Our faith was very small, but we felt really humbled when a year later on a return to the central village of Pangaluru thirty five converted Hindu men and women were baptized in the river as they confessed their faith in the Lord Jesus Christ. Some of these people had been converted the first time that they heard the gospel on our previous visits to the villages.

On the train for the long journey back to Madras, and then the flight home I was reminding my heart of the word of Paul to the Colossian Christians in Co. 1:16. 'All over the word this gospel is producing fruit and growing.' I had certainly been privileged yet again to experience that the Bible with its life transforming gospel is relevant in any part of the world, and in any culture or language.

11

Radio and Television

Through the years, there have been many opportunities to see if 'Have Bible-Will Travel' is equally effective over the radio waves, both terrestrial and by satellite. It began for me over 25 years ago with an invitation to participate in a Radio Worldwide Programme called 'Personally Speaking.' This meant writing and recording a series of Bible Studies that went out around the world on a daily basis. I remember in those early days receiving a letter from a man in Madagascar saying that he listened to my radio messages. I was greatly helped at this time by the TWR staff on how to write for radio, and many of their lessons I have been able to put into practice over the years.

My next introduction to Radio was with United Christian Broadcasters, and for six years I was able to share the weekly 'The Bible Speaks Today' programmes with my colleague Derek Cleave. At the same time I was invited to be a 'Radio preacher' with Good News Broadcasting. This entailed writing and recording a number of series of short Bible Studies consisting of five messages per week for their 'Bible Focus' programme. These with the UCB programmes are transmitted all over Europe. GNBA also asked me to contribute to their 'Bringing the Bible Alive' series.

Sitting in a radio studio and talking to the microphone as a 'person sitting across the room' to me, has been an interesting experience and a great privilege. I greatly enjoy this ministry. Thank God that radio can reach areas of the world that cannot be touched by normal missionary activity. There is always a sense of amazement at the way in which the modern use of radio by satellite, reaches the hearts of people maybe living in isolation in some remote part of the world. I still continue with this radio opportunity to reach people with God's Word that otherwise might never have any opportunity to hear God's message of salvation.

Television

After a visit to Newcastle to speak at the Grammar School I was invited to speak on the local Television Station. One of the staff who taught Religious Education and Rugby, ran a very successful Christian Union in the school. The lunchtime meeting had most of the sixth form present. It was a remarkable and effective evangelistic outreach and I was invited back a number of times. On one such visit the teacher told me that he had just been recording a series of epilogues for Tyne Tees Television. The Director for Religious Television was very sympathetic towards evangelical speakers and would I be interested if he gave me an invitation. My reply was an immediate 'Yes.' Within a couple of weeks the invitation came, asking me if I would start by writing 5 talks and then coming to Newcastle to record them in the studios of Tyne Tees Television.

The programmes were only 4 minutes at the end of each evening between 10-30 -11-30 pm. Writing for that length of time is much harder than writing for longer programmes. Feeling very scared, I set off for Newcastle for the first recording session, in what was a very unfamiliar situation as far as I was concerned. In those days there was no auto-cue for these Christian programmes, so it was a matter of memorising five programmes and speaking straight to camera. Later on auto-cue was provided and this made things a little easier. Having make up applied was also a new experience! Hurrying out of the Television Centre after recording my first series of five programmes,to go and speak in a Newcastle Secondary Modern School, I was stopped by the doorman who told me that I still had my make up on! I tried to imagine what the boys would have said if the visiting speaker had turned up complete with a face that was more suitable for a colour TV studio than a classroom!

I made a mess of my first programme, in fact I had to do it twice, but the director told me not to worry as the Bishop of Durham had taken six attempts at his first programme! When I felt more relaxed recording I really began to enjoy the opportunity that this gave me to bring the gospel, in I trust a relevant way, to people that would never have been reached in a normal evangelistic meeting. The director of the programmes was most helpful with supplying visual aids and props from time to time. In fact on one occasion he said to me that he preferred evangelicals to record this programme. He said that he enjoyed listening to a person who believed what he said, and not as he described them as 'wishy washy' people who tell us what they don't believe! We became good friends and he always took me out for lunch after the recording was finished.

During the next few years until Tyne Tees Television cut out the Christian slot, I was able to write and record 50 such programmes. On one occasion I asked the Religious Programmes Director how he started in this job. He told me that he had applied for the job as a news presenter but after the camera test they told him that he looked too much like Dracula, but would he like the job as Religious Director!

I was never able to see any of my programmes live so wondered what might be the possibility of doing something similar for the BBC. Watching a very poor programme late one evening I felt so cross at what I felt was a very pathetic Christian message that I sat down the next day and wrote four short scripts and sent them off to Birmingham. Two days later I received a letter inviting me to come across to Birmingham and meet the director of religious programmes.

Sitting in his office drinking a cup of coffee, he said that he was interested in what I had written, but that I could not say something that I had put in one of the scripts. I asked him what it was and his reply was that you cannot say that Jesus is the only way to God.(And this was 25 years ago!) I had a moment of inspiration so said to him, 'But I didn't say it. Jesus said it, so your problem is with him and not with me.' He sat there puzzled for a moment and then said, 'Okay, write a fifth script and come across again and record all five. Sadly, though I was able to write and record other programmes the powers that be at the BBC decided that there would be no more late night epilogues.

There have been other opportunities for Christian Television. During the time of Christian Ministries it was possible to write and produce two evangelistic films using the expertise of the Christian Television Association, in Bulgaria and the Czech Republic. Both of them in the language of the countries concerned. While we were filming in Prague, the secretary of the 'Church of the Brothers' asked us if we could make a short film in English to publicise a wonderful opportunity that they now had as a result of the freedom that had recently come to their country. Under the law of restitution, all land that had been confiscated by the communist regime was to be returned to its rightful owner. The church had been given back a plot of land on the outskirts of the city. We were taken to see the site and film it, then invited the president of the church to say on camera what their vision was for the future on this site..

Since 1991 the Evangelical Theological Seminary had been using rented space at the Cirkev Bratska Church in Prague, which served its' purpose for a limited number of students. More room was needed to expand this vision.

Crawford Telfer, our cameraman, put together a 10 minute film and we were able to give the church a master copy plus 50 copies on video. Returning to Prague five years later Audrey and myself were taken to see what had been done on the site, just a few yards from a Metro Station in Prague 9. The first thing we saw was a four storey seminary building. It has a lecture hall seating 80, a library, plus other rooms for classrooms and office space. In the building was also an apartment for the Director. Also on the same site was a rehabilitation unit that had been built for people who had suffered a stroke – and with a first class medical director. In addition they were just finishing building a home for old people that would accomodate 50 people. It was so encouraging to see what one short film was able to accomplish in raising money for such a strategic project. Yes, the Bible does travel well via Radio and Television.

Producing Missionary films for UFM Worldwide

During much of my evangelistic ministry, I have been privileged to serve on the Council of what was previously known as the Unevangelised Fields Mission, or UFM Worldwide as it is called today. Having been converted through the ministry of a Chinese doctor and spending my first year as a Christian in South East Asia, I have always had a love of mission and cross cultural communication. One of the lovely things about being on the staff of both M.W.E and Christians Ministries was that there was always the encouragement to work with existing mission agencies and so it was a great delight when UFM invited me to join their council. Wanting to bring missionary communication into the 20th century, I suggested that we should move into producing missionary video films in the countries where UFM was working. Having made the suggestion, I then was given the challenge to work with the Christian Television Association, and heading up this project that was subsequently going to take me from South America to Papua New Guinea.

Cote D'Ivoire

This is the new name for what was called the Ivory Coast, and this was to be my first country to visit with a camera crew. The objective was to see what God was doing, and the impact of the gospel in that land. It was a hot humid day in 1927 when a ship anchored off the Ivory Coast town of Sassandra. Several French missionaries from the 'Mission Biblique' disembarked into canoes and were safely rowed ashore. Basing themselves first of all in the town, they began to preach the gospel and then as a church was established they slowly moved up north. By 1929-30 they had reached the Youraba region and found that this particular tribe were very receptive to the gospel. They stayed and won many for Christ in the villages scattered throughout the area.

French is the language of commerce and education, and much of the evangelism and Bible teaching is done in the French language. There are also the tribal groups -64 of them, each with their own language, customs and culture, and only six of them with the whole Bible in their own language.

On this my first visit to Africa and to this country, it was encouraging to discover a training College for evangelists and also a Bible Institute for the training of pastors not only for this country but also for other French speaking African countries. Most towns seemed to have a church with an evangelical witness and there appeared to be freedom to preach throughout the country. Open air meetings, literature distribution, children's and teenager camps were organised and gospel films such as the 'Jesus' film were available and widely screened.

Both Government and local officials generally speaking were kindly disposed towards churches and land was available where churches could be built. Even on the road when stopped by police or customs, the gospel stickers on the car were enough to get a wave, and on one occasion the customs official said, 'Drive on, man of God!'-and they never say that to me at Heathrow!

There are still vast areas of the country that seem to be completely unreached with the Gospel. Start from any reasonably sized town and drive for two hours and you will pass dozens of villages whose inhabitants have never heard the name of Jesus.

It was in Sassandra, where the first missionaries landed those many years ago, that I met Francis Paton who along with his wife had worked in the town for many years. Francis took me to visit many of the beach people's villages(the Neyo tribe) and we found only three believers. To the west of Sassandra and again near the beaches, live the Krumen tribe- all 17,000 of them —again without any gospel witness as far as we could discover.

Inland we discovered vast areas of rubber and nut plantations, each of them totally self contained with thousands of workers and their families.' Please send an evangelist or pastor,' said the French Director of one such plantation.

Islam is a growing influence in this country.The largest Mosque in West Africa is in Yamoussokro near to the Bible Institute. In Gagnoa, ten minutes' walk from the evangelical church are two large mosques and two more are being constructed.

One fascinating opportunity was given to me at a ladies convention rally organised by one of the resident lady missionaries.There were hundreds present and they sat down on the ground in tribal groups. I preached in English and that was translated into French and at the same time into two tribal languages – but everybody listened with great attention. In the middle of my message I noticed that over on one side some ladies were placing what looked like a sheet in front of another lady. Suddenly there was a cry –the good lady had just given birth to a baby boy! The next moment she was sitting up and feeding the new born baby. It could only happen in Africa!

Travelling round the country and seeing the opportunities for the gospel, when we were editing the film on our return to England, our cameraman suggested a title. 'The Door's not open –it's off its hinges.' Sadly things can quickly change. There has now been a civil war in the country. North against South. Missionaries have had to leave. Bible Colleges have closed. The School for missionaries children is no longer open. Some African pastors have suffered much, and churches have been closed or attacked. However the church still stands firm and is growing, but it does stand in need of our prayers. Down in Sassandra with the help of some men from Northern Ireland with building skills the Bible school has been completed with rooms for lectures plus accommodation for students. What has happened in Cote D'Ivoire is a solemn reminder that we must, in the words of Jesus 'Work while it is day, for the night comes when no man can work.'

Gabon

On the west coast of Africa and straddling the equator is the little country of Gabon with just one million inhabitants. A former French colony, it received its independence from France in 1960 and after several early upheavals and a military coup, it is now a fairly stable one party state under its President Bongo —yes that really was his name!

It is a land of dense forests that cover some three quarters of the land mass, although from time to time the lush tropical rain forest gives way in parts to Savannah plains. Settlements spring up along the banks of the many rivers and some larger towns also have come into being as the years have gone by, although as you can imagine, none of them have a large population.

Missionary work can be traced back as far as 1845. There have been workers from the North American Christian and American Missionary Alliance working in the south since 1935. The former Africa Evangelical Fellowship had a couple workers working in the North, but otherwise we could find no other missionary input.

UFM Worldwide had been invited by the Gabon Christian Alliance church in the country, to consider sending missionaries to work with them.

Two members of the UFM Council(one of them a French speaking former missionary from Cote D'Ivoire and myself) were sent to see what the situation was, and the possibility for missionaries going to work with them.

From a welcome meeting of over 1200 believers just one hour after getting off the plane from France, to the final Sunday morning with a tribal congregation in Moanda, it was a kaleidoscope of sights, sounds, food, travel, jungle meetings (six in one day) and a 14-18 hour day.

After a quick internal flight to Tchibanga in the south we then climbed into a battered Toyota four wheel drive pick –up truck, for 1500 miles of bone shattering travel around the south on the dusty, bumpy roads. I was able to see something of the growth of the church in some areas as godly pastors had laboured with the gospel deep into the rain forest. In other areas we travelled all day, mile after mile, and village after village where the gospel has yet to go. One pygmy village that we visited was totally deserted by the time we arrived – it may have been our fault with our white faces!

Government officials were met (seven in all) and we were also granted an audience with the governor of Franceville who then invited us to his residence for liquid refreshment! So what were my impressions of this lightening visit ? First of all here was the National African Church with a great heart for evangelism and outreach to the unevangelised. Secondly, here was a church with a need for good solid Bible teaching so that they could establish the 18,000 known believers in their faith.

Opportunity

The church leaders gave us the Macedonian call,'Come over and help us.'Visas and resident permits were possible and the opportunity is there to work with the National Church.

Gabon has a high literacy rate that is possibly the highest in Africa and although there are dozens of tribal groups, all education and commerce is undertaken in the French language. With only a million inhabitants there is a glorious opportunity to reach a nation for Christ if we could only take up this challenge.

On the long train journey up from the south, through the great forest and across many rivers,I was rejoicing that I had once again seen that the Bible travels with its life transforming message into any culture, but I also had a heavy heart.Before saying farewell to our African brethren we had to tell them that we do not have missionaries queuing up at home and waiting to go. But I did promise them that I would do my best, my very best, to put the challenge of Gabon to our evangelical churches in Great Britain and see if God would call out a team of workers who would be ready to get up and go with the gospel to Gabon.

It was not possible to take a camera team to produce a video film on this a first visit, but I did manage to put together an audio visual programme on the Challenge of Gabon – but sadly from many screenings in different churches in our country there has been to date no one coming forward to serve God in Gabon.

Going for Gold in Brazil

In the town of Sierra Pelada, 500 miles south from the mouth of the river Amazon, just 20 years ago, a cowhand discovered a gold nugget. News travelled rapidly and two weeks later 10,000 gold diggers from all over Brazil had arrived in a frantic search for gold. It speedily became a vast open top mine in which as many as 40,000 dug for gold.

But there is another 'gold' in Brazil that is of far greater value, and that is the 125 million inhabitants from a 'melting pot of races' that live in this, the largest country in South America.

For well over a 100 years the gospel has been in this land, and since 1931 UFM Worldwide have been working for God mainly in the north of the country and particularly in the vast Amazon basin. It was at their invitation that I visited this country on to two occasions. The main objective of the visits was to see something of the power of the gospel in peoples lives through missionary witness, and also to see something of the challenge of the Street kids of Brazil. On both occasions it was with cameraman Crawford Telfer of the 'Christian Television Association' that two films were produced.

Early missionaries worked amongst the Indian tribes who live on the rivers and in the interior. In fact, in the early days there were three missionaries martyred by the Kayapo Indians. Subsequently that tribe was reached with the gospel as were other tribal groups. Today the Indian tribes put together would only number about 110,000.

By comparison it was fascinating to discover that here in Brazil live the largest number of Japanese outside of Japan —in the Amazon basin two million and in the whole of Brazil possibly 10 million. If ever there was a hidden people group, it must surely be these Japanese people.

Fifty six percent of the population of Brazil now live in urban areas, and San Paulo will be the largest city in the world within the next ten years, although some of the larger Chinese cities have possibly outgrown this number.

Bible College and Theological training is important for the future of the church in Brazil, and it was thrilling to be present on graduation day at the San Louis Seminary and to see fine young Brazilian young people going out to serve the Lord in their own country.

Youth work is highlighted in a uniformed organisation know as the 'Jet Cadets,' with ranks based upon the Brazilian Airforce. Honour badges are won for Bible memory work and for completing up to seven Bible Correspondence courses.

In Maraba on the Trans Amazon Highway I was able to preach in a new church being planted, and also in the city of Manaus the capital on the river Amazon. Manaus is 1,200 miles up the river and with a temperature of 41 degrees and a humidity to match I was expected to preach wearing a jacket, shirt and tie! I had to tell the missionary that I did not have a jacket with me. None of his fitted me, but he did loan me a tie. There was a power failure during the service and by the time I had finished preaching and walking to the door to shake hands with the congregation my feet were feeling as if I was walking on water – the sweat was running down my legs and into my shoes!

I was due to come home from Brazil just before Christmas, flying from Belem at the mouth of the Amazon to Recife on the coast. However the Brazillian airline Varig had gone on strike and there was no way of getting to Recife and catching my connection by Air France to Paris and then London.

But a very resourceful missionary said that she thought that there was a bus from Belem that leaves Friday afternoon and gets to Recife on Sunday afternoon and there might be a seat on it. There was, but my idea of a coach turned out to be a bus! Yes, there was one spare seat so I paid for the ticket and clambered on board. It was some journey with not a very comfortable seat and stifling hot. It did stop about every four hours, and the Brazilian passengers got off to buy food – the inevitable beans that Brazillians love so much! I had been warned not to buy food at wayside food stalls, but I could buy cold cans of coca cola. By the time I did eventually arrive at Recife I felt a bit like Michelin man and could not face another coke for months.

My inability to speak any Portuguese was a problem, and I was feeling rather isolated until I noticed at one stop an old man sitting near the front of the bus was walking up and down the aisle and handing out leaflets. In his hand was also a small book and as he reached my seat I could see that on the cover was a cross. He was handing out gospel tracts. I said to him 'Hallelujah' and pointed skywards, and he grabbed me and jabbered away in Portuguese. He then managed to get another passenger to change seats with him and so he sat with me for the rest of the long journey. Every time the bus stopped he wanted to buy me some food but I had to politely say 'no thank you.' He was God's provision for me on the unexpected long bus journey.

I certainly saw Brazil as I had never seen it before, but on the journey I was thanking God that He had not called me to Brazil as a missionary, though I could not remember a missionary that I had met over the past weeks who would have been anywhere else in the world than Brazil. The reason is that when you are in the will of God then in the words of Romans 12 it is 'good, pleasing and acceptable.'

I was told in Brazil, that the Christian church in the country grows faster than the birth rate, but there does seem to be a great need for good solid Bible teaching to establish these many new believers in their faith. As in Gabon in West Africa, the Bible and its great message of salvation and forgiveness travels well in this vast country.

To the edge of the world

To the north of Australia lies the second largest Island in the world. One half is Irian Jaya or Papua as it is now called and the other Papua New Guinea, and it was in PNG that I was to spend a month with a camera team from Christian Television Association making a film for UFM Worldwide. A former Australian colony, it is now an independent country with a population of 3 million, split into 750 tribal groups each with its own language.

Missionary work can be traced back to 1875, but it was only after World War Two in the Pacific came to an end, that hundred of missionaries came to this majestic country. They sought to bring the gospel to these remote tribes people who seem to have remained in a time warp that is very much stone age. With the birth of the Missionary Aviation Fellowship hundreds of previously inaccessible tribes are now reachable. Missionaries could now stay on location and work with the people and be supplied from the air by MAF.

The razorback mountains forming the spine of the Island had shielded these tribes people from the outside world, Even three decades after man had stepped on the surface of the moon, there were still many who had never left their small valley that is called home, set amongst the 4694 metre high peaks.

Our journeys for the most part were in the light Cessna aircraft of MAF, and we flew with them 15 times during the month. I never ceased to be amazed at the skill and expertise of these dedicated pilots as they took off and landed on jungle airstrips or beside swampy lagoons. Bouncing in the turbulence just above the clouds, looking for a hole through which we could descend, or flying through some of the valleys between the mountains was a hair-raising experience. I must confess that there were times when me eyes were kept tightly closed.

Down on the ground we first went to Tari in the Western Highlands. This was the home of the Huli tribe. The Huli men are short and stocky, and wear very little apart from a great wig made up of brilliant bird feathers and flowers. With tattooed, painted faces they look very fierce indeed. Tari is also the Headquarters of the Evangelical Church of Papua. It was formed in 1966 and unites together over 14,000 believers from 36 different tribal groups.(While writing this I have just heard that a MAF plane coming in to land at Tari has crashed, killing two pilots and seriously injuring two passengers.)

From Tari, we flew due west to near the Indonesian border. On the banks of the Wai Maeri river is Rumginae, and this is the site of the missionary hospital that serves the whole area. Melanesian people always associate sickness with the spiritual, so at such times they are particularly open to the Gospel. In fact the National Church would say that 35% of the current church membership were first reached with the gospel through the medical care given them when they were sick. I remember hearing a Papuan man standing on the verandah of his hospital ward and giving his testimony. He was telling the people listening to him as he pointed to the scar on his bare stomach and saying 'The doctors mended my stomach, but God mended my heart.'

Our other form of transport from Rumginae was the dugout canoe with an outboard motor, and I speedily discovered that I was not built for such means of transport! But it did mean that we were able to visit and film other tribal groups up the many rivers. On this trip we were able to take some of the first copies of a part of the New Testament to one tribal group. As soon as our box of Scriptures were unloaded from the canoe, the men sat down and began reading out loud the Word of God. As they were reading they were saying the same phrase over and over again. When I asked the missionary to tell me what they were saying he said, 'they are saying God speaks to us in our own language.' It was a sight and a sound that I will not easily forget. What a vivid reminder of the power of the written Word of God in peoples lives.

From Rumginae we flew southward to Mapodo and then down to Balimo and the swampy lagoon country. In this part of the country you always walk with your eyes looking at the ground —snakes abound and they are deadly.

It was after 34,000 miles of travel and a multitude of experiences, feelings and food that it was time for home. I did have a lovely bonus at the end of the trip. It was to stay on for a further ten days and give the Bible readings at two conferences for missionaries of the Asia Pacific Mission.

Please don't send me to Africa!

I want to take you to one more country. The Amazon was hot and sticky. Papua New Guinea was fascinating with hundreds of different tribes. Spain and Portugal were just a quick flight across the channel, and Cote' D'Ivoire in West Africa was enjoyable. However I must confess that I did not want to go to Zaire(Republic of the Congo as it is now known) in the heart of Africa. Like a number of African countries, it was in a desperate state both politically and economically. It had such a high inflation rate that its currency was practically worthless. This was to be another trip with camera man Crawford Telfer and to produce another film for UFM Worlwide. Twice before we had aborted the trip because of the turmoil in the country, but this time the missionary task force in Kisangani in the centre of the country gave the all clear that it was safe to go- the soldiers had just been paid their wages-six months late!

Two weeks of travel by MAF in a five seater plane, Cessna, dug out canoe on the mighty Congo river, hours of spine jarring journeys in a battered Land Rover, plus being the hottest month of the year, all combined to make it a never —to-be-forgotten experience.

The political situation was such that you were liable to be stopped at army checkpoints – and we were on a number of occasions. Filming was hazardous, so a government 'minder' was required – at only $5 a day. He was worth his weight in gold, rescuing us from all kinds of difficult situations. We christened him 'James Bond,' he even turned up for breakfast at the missionaries' house every morning.He was hungry as were most of the population. In fact most government employees had not been paid for months and you wonder just how anybody manages to survive. It is no wonder that there is so much bribery, corruption and crime.

Kisangani, where we were based, was the former Stanleyville during the Colonial rule of Belgium. Around this area during the Simba rebellion of 1964 thirty missionaries and children were brutally murdered. From Kisangana we visited other centres down river and in the rain forest. One morning we flew over 600 miles of jungle and were glad that our single engined Cessna kept going. Sitting in the co-pilots seat I asked the Australian Pilot what would happen if the propeller stopped, and his calm reply was – six minutes to the trees! We met at this time only five missionaries living and serving God in this vast area of Congo and four of them were women! I could not help thinking, where are the men for this great task ?

Congo churches are good at evangelism and during the dry season a number of evangelistic teams go out weekly to preach the gospel in unevangelised areas. There is a desperate need for good Bible teaching for the thousands of new believers. Bible school teachers, nurses, doctors and evangelists are still needed. It was to record on film some of these needs and opportunities than thankfully we were able to come back with 7 hours of film.

In addition to the filming, the Bishop of Kisangana invited me to preach in the Cathedral. When you have 800 Africans singing their hearts out, plus a number of different choirs,then you have been closest to Heaven that you can get on earth! After the Sunday services, Bishop Asani then invited me to speak at the Pastors' conference that followed on the Monday, and then to the youth of the church in the evening.

The Republic of the Congo is a country with very great problems politically and tribally. The church has suffered much but it still continues to grow. There is no question but that the Bible has travelled well in this country. Looking back on my many travels over the past 50 years, the word of Paul in Colossians 1:6 rings true. All over the world this gospel is bearing fruit and growing just as it has been doing among you since the day you heard and understood God's grace in all its truth.'

12

The Gospel in a Pagan Culture

It has been a great privilege to travel to so many countries of the world with my Bible and its life transforming message. It has also been an encouragement and challenge to see something of the ministry of evangelism through national churches and evangelists reaching their own people with the gospel. Now as I spend most of my time in my own country, my constant concern is how can we bring the gospel to our pagan culture, because in the last decade the situation has changed radically.

At the beginning of my ministry as an evangelist, the pattern was fairly straight forward. Most of our population had at least some knowledge of the Bible as far as well known stories in the Old and New Testament were concerned. Religious education was the experience of all infant and junior age groups. Sunday schools were reasonably well attended.

Twenty five years ago, three of us who had been on the staff of the 'Movement for World Evangelisation' came together as a team, calling ourselves 'Christian Ministries – God's Word for Today's World' John Blanchard, Derek Cleave and myself had all been on the staff of NYLC prior to

MWE, so we had been together for many years. Although we were a team it did not mean that we spent all of our time together, for we had the freedom to pursue individual ministries. Through the pages of this book I have shared something of how that freedom led me to many parts of the world.

However now back in my own country where I started my evangelistic ministry fifty years ago the future presented a great challenge. Looking back into our history as a nation there was a time when people lived, worked and shared in a very close knit society, and they certainly communicated with each other by talking and in other ways.

The industrial revolution almost swept away the community based, rural lifestyle. People moved in their thousands from their old safe communities to the growing urban areas and I think that generally speaking people now live in areas where their neighbours were not necessarily the people they worked with during the day. To all of this were added long working hours, and time consuming travel to work and home again. People became isolated in their homes.

Later came the advent of radio followed by television. All this meant that communication that had been between people who knew each other, now came into the home via the media. Add to this the growing use of the internet so that person to person interaction has almost disappeared. Possibly as many as 80% of the British Population now live in urbanised areas where community to a large extent has been obliterated.

As evangelists working in the new British culture we began to ask ourselves questions about the success of the kind of evangelism that we had engaged in for many years. How many non-Christian people were coming into what was then the format for evangelistic outreach? Meetings were centred round a public meeting each night for a week or two, and sometimes in the summer months maybe up to four weeks in a Tent.

If you had good publicity and a fascinating programme, other churches might support, but we were beginning to feel that most Christians were only coming along to enjoy the meetings. As time went on many Christians were unwilling to come out and support such meetings. Added to this, the fact is that there is a dearth of Biblical knowledge and false theology abounds. Morals are at an all time low and communication with people is increasingly difficult. However having said this I am convinced that a church needs to have a programme of evangelism throughout the year. A special proclamation of the gospel to people, whether for a period of a number of days or even a 'one off' event has a number of advantages.

A special outreach for a limited period gives a sense of urgency to the task, and it certainly stimulates and focuses prayer. It reminds the church that evangelism is the responsibility of the whole church and not just the leaders. It gives an extra impetus to invite non- Christian friends and neighbours because of the special nature of what is happening. It should involve all areas of the life of the church and produce fellowship at a deeper level, and there is no greater fellowship than that of service together in the cause of the gospel. It certainly challenges the church with regard to its real contact with the outside world, and of course it gives the church a means of evaluation. But above all, if there is no other reason it is obedience to the great commission.

At this point we began to look at a number of areas. First of all what were the hindrances to unconverted people coming under the sound of the gospel ? Were we, the people of God part of the problem? Were the premises that we invited them to come into not very helpful, and then the programme was usually outside the realm of understanding to the man in the street. To be given a hymn book and told that we were going to sing a hymn a stanza of which is 'The Hill of Zion yields a thousand sacred sweets,' your guest might wonder if they were 'Bounty Bars or Kit Kat! Were there any insights that we had missed or ignored ? What methods could we use that

Would involve church members more personally in being participators in evangelism rather that spectators.

At this point we were totally committed to both the message and the method. The message being the gospel and the method preaching. Jesus said to His disciples 'Go and preach,' and in the Acts of the Apostles is a record of their obedience to the command of Jesus. Preaching,I believe is always relevant for all time and in any culture. However the context in which you do preach possibly needs to change.

Four words now seemed to spell out a different context and they were the words,food, homes,occupations and hobbies. All unconverted people are familiar with at least 2 or 3 things. They rarely if ever attend church, but all unconverted people eat! Jesus often ministered in homes. When Matthew was converted he organised a feast at his house when Jesus was present and spoke. Paul in Colossians 1 said that, 'we should be given to hospitality.'

How do you start ? Ideally with a blank sheet of paper, and on it list the potential of your church in terms of personnel. Men and women, young and old, occupations, hobbies, sports etc. What contact do your church members have in the community. For example, school governors, teachers, doctors, probation officers, workers in social services. How many members live within walking distance of the church. The priority for evangelism ought to start with those that we already know and not complete strangers.

Sunday is not usually the best day for evangelism, but if you do use it make sure that the time of the event is suitable for the people you want to reach.Members are encouraged to open their homes for coffee,tea, refreshments, luncheons, suppers, dinner parties etc. Invitations should be personal on attractively designed invitation cards with RSP requested. Business people could arrange something special for colleagues. It is always important to make sure that after the meal there is to be a talk on a Christian topic such as is 'Christianity relevant for today?' But of course, special subjects can be tackled for special audiences.

All present at these events are there by personal invitation, so people are more likely to stay talking after the programme is concluded. This can be a great opportunity for church members more personally to be participators in evangelism rather than spectators.

So what are the advantages of this kind of evangelism you may ask ? First of all, unconverted people are reached with the gospel. The majority of those present at every event are non-Christians. No Christian is expected to come without a guest or guests. Church members have to be involved on a personal level. You can have a personalised prayer list of people who will be present at various events. Smaller prayer meetings during the day or at the same time as the event is taking place means that friends can be prayed for, and sometimes even as they are listening to the gospel. The church will certainly have a lot of fresh contact with your community and have made good friends within your community.

Some examples of such evangelistic opportunities

House meetings can be in any size of house or locality. Homes can be used for special invitation dinners. For larger events, a Men's dinner is nearly always successful. Men respond to an invitation better on their own rather than with their wives. However, you must not leave the ladies out, so a candlelight supper for them would be a good idea. If your church is located near to a shopping area, then you could have a business trader's dinner. One church that I worked with arranged such a dinner, and invited local traders to be guests of the church. It so happened that the mayor of the city owned one of these shops, and said that he would be delighted to come and bring his wife. He added that he would make it an official mayoral visit. I was due to speak that night after the dinner and the Mayor and his wife sat beside me on the top table. It was the first time that I had to start my message for the evening with 'My Lord Mayor and Lady Mayoress.' What was interesting was that the mayor came back to the church on the following Sunday morning as an ordinary member of the congregation.

Foreign food is also useful, and in most cities there are an abundance of Chinese and Indian Restaurants. If they have a separate banquet facility it is possible to hire it for an evening and bargain for a set price (Buffet meal being a good idea.) I was invited to speak at one where the restaurant only charged £6 a head. I also remember a Bangledeshi Balti house where the waiters came in and listened to the message. This was followed the next evening in a Chinese restaurant with a Chinese banquet for young adults.

Original opportunities

One young lady working as a secretary in an architects practice told her boss that she would arrange a buffet lunch to be brought into the office.He agreed, and the whole staff (7 of them) had lunch and then listened to the gospel. When the time ran out the boss said, 'carry on for another 15 minutes' Just down the road from another church was a primary school, and they invited the staff to stay after school and the church would provide a strawberry and cream tea. After tea there was a twenty minute talk on 'Is Christianity Relevant in Education Today.' A most challenging opportunity was to sit on a high stool in the school kitchen and talk to the dinner ladies as they ate their lunch after finishing serving the children.

In Guildford, one lady in the church was the secretary to the Commandant of the Fire Officers Training College. Evidently, after a busy day they would relax over a nice dinner and then retreat to the bar for the evening. Very bravely she asked her boss if it would be possible to have me come and speak after dinner on 'Is Christianity Relevant in Today's World' He agreed, and I drove out to the College in fear and trembling, wondering how the message would be received. I needn't have worried, they gave me a good hearing and then questions followed that went on for a long time. One chief fire officer from Liverpool said to me, 'now I know what my son means because he keeps telling me that he has been born again.' Evidently his son was a member of a church youth group and was a member of a Bible study group that met every week on a Sunday afternoon.

Being in Bangor in Northern Ireland we found that the DHSS offices were right next door to the Baptist Church. On some of the week days during the mission, the church offered jacket potatoes with different fillings freely available in the church lounge at lunch time followed by the gospel. We must have had most of the DHSS staff during the week.

Maybe one of the most amusing evenings was a special supper for the Bromley Cat Club. Two the ladies in the church were members of this club. They invited 20 other ladies to come for supper and then for me to speak. One evening in Ilfracombe, I was speaking at a buffet supper at the Post Office Social Club. It happened because one of the members of the church who was a postman asked if the church could provide a buffet supper at the club, after which I would speak. At the same time my colleague John Blanchard was speaking at a dinner for dentists' in the home of a Christian dentist from the church.

There have been events on skin care, keep fit and make up! I did think at the time that somebody was dropping hints by inviting me to speak at these! In this same church a number of the members were school governors, so a dinner was arranged to which the governors were invited. Something similar happened when the wife of the minister of the church who was a local magistrate invited her colleagues to a dinner just for them. Cake decorating demonstrations are usually well attended, and I remember speaking after a demonstration of Japanese flower arranging because a Japanese student studying at the University attended the church. A photographic club in Colchester had the pastor as a member of the club. It was not difficult for him to invite them to come to dinner at the church to watch an audio visual of one of my many visits to Czechoslavakia and then to listen to the gospel after eating a very nice meal prepared by the ladies of the church.

A special supper for traffic wardens was certainly special. As was a dinner for British Telecom managers and then a lunchtime meal for the

Directors of the Anglia Building Society. One memorable Saturday morning I spoke at a House meeting in Dunstable. Among those present was the Moslem owner of a restaurant just down the road, plus the wife of the BBC director of the Winter Olympics. She had met her husband when she was singing in opera in Manchester.

Derek Cleave, one of my colleagues has been chaplain of Bristol City Football club for over 25 years. When we were holding a mission in his home church in Bristol, he planned a special invitation dinner for the club in the church hall. Recently having been redecorated and set out, the church ladies prepared a first class dinner one Monday evening. Derek then invited the whole playing staff, management and office staff to be guests for the evening – with after dinner speaker John Blanchard. Sixty players and staff accepted the invitation and it was a great audience to listen to the Gospel. John must have spoken for 40 minutes and there was rapt attention. Every player was then given a copy of John's book 'Right with God.' It could have been an embarrassing evening if Derek had not noticed that the ladies had put the serviettes out in the colours of Bristol Rovers. Derek noticed it in time and a quick rush across to a nearby shop bought the right colours before the guest arrived!

If God has given you contact with any particular group of people, young or old, then it should not be too difficult to ask them to be your guest at a function great or small. I think that you might be pleasantly surprised how many of your neighbours, friends or workmate would accept such an invitation from you to be your guest. Of course you must always make it clear that after the dinner or supper that there will be a guest speaker giving a talk on 'Is the Christian Faith Relevant in Today's World.' Such a subject it non-threatening and this or any other subject is best put in the form of a question.

I believe that all of these situations I have mentioned illustrate the need to put the never changing Gospel into a different context. The context of what could be best described as 'Hospitality Evangelism.' The Bible and the gospel message is still relevant in the pagan world of today. Our country is full of people who at the moment are as the Bible puts it, 'dead in trespasses and sin.' It is to such people that we must go and provide a context in which they can hear this life transforming message of the gospel of the Lord Jesus Christ. So why don't you get involved in this kind of evangelism.

13

The Message is the Same

Fifty two years ago during a two week Tent Mission in Lowhill, Wolverhampton, I preached for the first time as a full time evangelist and I believe that this message still travels well in the world today. So as I end this book, I want to close with the same message that I preached those many years ago, because it is all about God's salvation in Jesus Christ.

When you examine the Christian faith in the Bible you will discover that it uses the word 'saved' or 'salvation many times, but what does it mean? It is a word which we are very familiar with in every day language, and it has the thought of rescue, help and deliverance. It speaks of a need that can only be met from an outside source. The hungry of the world cry out for food in order to be saved from starvation. In some areas of the world there are still deadly diseases like malaria that kill thousands of people. Sadly, there are still some countries where people are slaves, and sold as such.

Whenever there is a disaster in some parts of the world, whether from earthquake, flood or famine, the more affluent nations of the world are usually urged to respond to help those who have no possibility of helping themselves. So we do understand what it means in these circumstances.

However what does it mean in the Christian sense? In a letter written by Paul to the Christians living in Rome, he uses this word and says,'If you confess with you mouth Jesus is Lord, and believe in your heart that God raised Him from the dead you will be saved.' However having read these words you may still be no nearer knowing what the Bible teaches when it speaks of being saved.

Before Jesus was born, an angel appeared to Joseph and gave him some important information about the baby that Mary was carrying. He told him that the child was going to be a boy, and that He was to be called Jesus. Then he was given the reason why this boy was to be so named. 'For He will save His people from their sins.' (Matt.1:21)

When the Bible uses the word 'saved' it is talking about salvation from our sins, and in case we might think that it is nothing to do with us, the Bible reminds us that,'All have sinned and come short of the glory of God.' (Rom.3:23) Sin is breaking God's law ie.'The Ten Commandments'- and any one of them. In fact the Bible goes on to say,'For whoever keeps the whole law and yet stumbles at just one point is guilty of breaking all of it.(James 2:10) Vague generalisations about sin are ineffective, we need specific admonitions and prohibitions and this is why God gave us His law. But sin is also omission, or failing to do positive good, for the Bible says that 'to him who knows to do good and doesn't do it, to him it is sin.' Jesus added one other condemnation when he said.'If you do not believe that I am the one I claim to be you will die in your sins.(John 8:24.)

Although we have been created by God and for Him, we have sadly left the path of obedience to God and stepped onto the path of personal independence from God. We have substituted God's government for self government, and that is sin. But without Him life makes no sense at all. On our own we are unable to change our nature as the sin principle dominates us, and our actions and habits show that we are in slavery to sin. We live our lives under the shadow of death. As human beings we were made by God and for God and He gave us a spiritual capacity. We are far from God, yet we constantly search for our spiritual home and for an experience which materialism is unable to give us. Our greatest need is for the forgiveness of sins and an experience of God's salvation.

Because we have rejected God and followed our own way rather than God's way we are guilty before Him. Guilt is both a feeling and a fact. It is a feeling because our consciences tell us that we have rebelled against Him. We deserve God's judgement and we need to be saved, delivered and rescued from that judgement.

So who can be saved?

First of all we are told clearly in the Bible what the scope of God's salvation is, for it says very definitely that 'Everyone who calls on the name of the Lord will be saved.' (Rom.10:13) No matter what colour or race, good or bad, religious or pagan, young or old. It does not matter whether you have a little knowledge of the Bible or a lot, the invitation is 'Everyone who calls will be saved.' The Bible says that 'God so loved the world that He gave His one and only Son, that whoever believes in Him shall not perish but have eternal life.' (John 3:16) Paul in Romans 10 v.12 says, 'The same Lord is rich unto all that call upon Him.' Peter writes in 2 Peter 3:9, 'God is not willing that any should perish, but that all should come to repentance.' In 2 Cor.5:19 Paul says, 'God was reconciling the world to Himself in Christ.' God's salvation is for the world and therefore it is for you. No one can turn round and say, 'But it cannot possibly be for me . . . ' To make such a statement is in effect to call God a liar, because He says that 'Everyone who calls upon the name of the Lord will be saved.'

The Lord is the Saviour

Paul then underlines the source of this salvation and forgiveness. There is no salvation in politics, or social reform or science, but only in Jesus Christ. It is not calling upon the name of the minister or priest. It is not calling upon the name of the church.It is calling upon the name of the Lord. Until the good news of salvation is received, a state of hostility exists between God and us.It is the death of Christ alone that can change our situation. It is the cross that satisfies God's justice,for there God's anger against sin was fully poured out upon Jesus as our substitute.The way is now open for us repentant sinners to 'call upon the name of the name of the Lord,' and so to receive the reconciliation and salvation made available for us in Jesus Christ. To save a single soul is beyond the combined resources of the world's banks or the skill of any top flight legal advocate, but if you call upon the name of the Lord you will be saved.

Some scientists believe that genetic manipulation holds promise for both the improvement and the destruction of human civilisation. By controlling genes which largely determine the physical and even mental characteristics of a person, the scientists hope that one day they can create the perfect man. But to control or alter the physical, even mental characteristics of a man is not enough to make a perfect man. For the Bible makes it quite clear that 'The heart of man is deceitful and desperately wicked.' At the heart of the human problem is the problem of the human heart, and only God can change us on the inside and give us a new heart.

Call upon the name of the Lord

Why does the Bible says, 'Call upon the name of the Lord.' In order to find an answer we must look at some verses in the Bible that will help us in our understanding of why this phrase is used. In the Acts of the Apostles and right at the beginning of the Christian gospel, Peter and John heal a lame man at the beautiful gate of the temple. In healing him, Peter says, 'In the name of Jesus Christ of Nazareth rise up and walk.(Acts 3:6.) Later on when they are challenged by the religious leaders as to how this miracle happened they said, 'In the name of Jesus Christ does this man stand here whole.' (Acts 4:10.) 'Neither is there salvation in any other, for there is none other name under Heaven given among men whereby we must be saved.'(Acts 4:13.) It was the late Lindsay Clegg who said that, 'There are many paths to Christ as there are feet to tread them, but there is only one way to God and that way is through Jesus Christ.'

Now there are number of reasons why the 'Name of the Lord' is so important. When you call upon the 'Name of the Lord,' you are calling upon God your creator and lawgiver and the one you have sinned against, for all sin is ultimately against God. But you are also calling upon the one whose name is Jesus. Do you remember what the angel said to Joseph about the baby that Mary was carrying? 'You will call His name Jesus, for He will save His people from their sins.' For the Lord Jesus Christ is the Saviour of sinners.

Another title given to Jesus is, the Christ, the Son of God, and the Bible often uses this title. Paul in Romans 5:8 says, 'But God commendeth His love towards us in that while we were yet sinners, Christ died for us.' John in 1 John 4:14 echoes this truth when he writes, 'The Father sent the Son to be the Saviour of the world.'' So you can trust Him and His promises for He is the Lord Jesus Christ.

But you have to call

It is very important to notice that this promise emphasises the importance of the 'Name of the Lord.' It is also very clearly tells us that in order to enjoy this salvation we have to call for it. If you have an illness in the middle of the night you may need to call a doctor. He certainly will not come if you don't telephone him and urge him to come and see you. If it is winter time and the pipes burst and water is spurting everywhere, you will need to phone for a plumber. If you car breaks down on the motorway and you have renewed your AA Subscription, then you can ring for help. There is no other way that the AA will come to your rescue until you call. Now although God's salvation is universal in the sense that it is offered to the world, it is never bestowed automatically, there has to be a call to God for it, and such a call is only made when there is a sense of need.

Jesus one day told a story about two men who prayed to God in the Jewish Temple because they wanted to be accepted by God. The first man was very religious and moral, and as he prayed he told God how good he was compared to other men. The second man was just the opposite sort of character. He was at the bottom of the pile as far as religion and personal goodness was concerned. He came and prayed what I think is possibly the easiest and yet the hardest prayer to pray. He cried to God and said, 'God be merciful to me a sinner.' (Luke 18:9-14) He wasn't interested in comparing himself with any other human being. He just realised that as far as God was concerned he was a sinner. He also knew that if there was to be mercy, forgiveness and salvation then only God could provide it, so he called, believing that God could and would have mercy upon him.

Jesus added a wonderful encouraging postscript to the story when he said that this second man went down to his house right with God, forgiven and saved. If at this moment you realise that you are a sinner and believe in your heart that Jesus Christ died for your sin on the cross, then call to Him to save you, and He will. He promises that 'Everyone who calls on the name of the Lord will be saved.'

There are so many people who believe the great truths of the Christian faith. They realise that they are sinners and even believe that Christ died for their sins and that He is the only way of salvation, but the tragedy is that they have never called and so they are still unsaved because they have only believed in an intellectual way. Could that still be true of you?

Salvation is guaranteed

The verse says very clearly that 'everyone who calls will be saved.' It doesn't say, might be saved, or even stands a good chance of being saved. It states very clearly and dogmatically 'will be saved.' Jesus said, 'Whoever hears my word and believes Him who sent me has eternal life and will not be condemned; he has crossed over from death to life.' (John 5:24.) God promises in the Bible that 'as far as the east is from the west, so far has he removed our transgressions from us.'(Psalm 103:12) If it had said 'as far as the north pole is from the south pole, ' we would not be happy, because it is possible to measure between them, but we cannot measure the distance between east and west poles.

Discovering and experiencing God's salvation in Jesus Christ brings reconciliation with God. You are not saved because you attend church, are confirmed or baptised. You are not even saved if you lead a respectable life or help your neighbour, but only if you have called upon the name of the Lord. Call to Him now, 'God be merciful to me a sinner,' and you will meet God and then be assured as C.H. Spurgeon said, 'it is not your hold on Christ that saves you, but rather His hold on you.'

So here is the challenge of the Gospel

The Bible says, 'if you confess with your mouth Jesus is Lord, and believe in your heart that God raised Him from the dead, you will be saved.For it is with your heart that you believe and it is with your mouth that you confess and are saved, for the Lord richly blesses all who call, for everyone who calls upon the name of the Lord will be saved.' (Romans 10:9-13.) —and this message travels well all over the world.

For the past 52 years it has been my unspeakable privilege to proclaim this great and glorious gospel of salvation. I can certainly say with the apostle Paul in Romans 1:16.'I am not ashamed of the gospel, because it is the power of God unto salvation for everyone who believes.